THE CHINA
GUANGDON(

U0613419

中国梦·广东故事

COMMON PROSPERITY

共享的广东

WANG HE

TRANSLATED BY JIN YANG

SPM
Southern Publishing & Media Co.Ltd.
Guangdong People's Publishing House Ltd.

Editors: Wang Ning, Shi Yong
Published by Guangdong People's Publishing House Ltd., China
www.gdpph.com

First published 2017
Printed in the People's Republic of China

The China Dream: Guangdong Story- Common Prosperity/ Wang He and translated by Jin Yang
ISBN 978-7-218-11892-5 (paperback, 1st edition)

Preface

Located in southern China, Guangdong Province is the first region in China to implement the reform and opening up, and it is also one of the most affluent areas nationwide. The Pearl River, China's third largest river, runs across the whole province. The Pearl River Delta is an alluvial plain flushed by the Pearl River. After nearly 40 years of rapid development, it has already become one of the most important city groups of China. The Hong Kong Special Administrative Region, and the Macao Special Administrative Region adjoin to Guangdong Province. With the natural geographical relations and the same cultural background, they constitute China's unique Guangdong—Hong Kong—Macao Greater Bay Area—a world—class vigorous economic and cultural area.

For nearly 40 years of rapid development, Guangdong has been playing a leading role in innovation, spurring the rapid development of new growth drivers. There are many rapidly grown—up enterprises in Guangdong, such as Huawei, Tencent, and UMi, which have become important engines of Guangdong's new economy development. Huawei and Tencent are now widely known in China. We try to approach such enterprises and their employees, to find the "secret" of the most innovative and cutting—edge development in Guangdong.

Guangdong has been the most dynamic foreign trade area in China since ancient times. And Guangzhou has been a commercial city through the ages, as well as an important interconnecting city alongside the "Maritime Silk Road". Foreigners from all over the world travel across major cities in Guangdong everyday, sightseeing, attending business meetings, studying or visiting friends. In Guangzhou, there are a large number of foreigners from Europe, America, Southeast Asia, the Middle East, Africa and other places, doing business here everyday. They ship back clothing, fabric, seafood, electrical appliances or glasses; foreign trade is booming. In the Shenzhen Special Economic Zone ports, people and vehicles travelling between Hong Kong and Shenzhen are always lined up. Foreigners living here for many years gradually adopt and merge into customs and culture of Guangdong, and regard Guangdong as their "second home". Meanwhile, tens of millions of workers from other provinces live in Guangdong, especially in the Pearl River Delta, where they work in factories, earn money to support their families, and try to realize their own dreams and ambitions. Whether foreigners or migrant workers, they are all practitioners, promoters and witnesses of Guangdong's reform and opening up. We conduct close observation of their work and life to record their ups and downs.

Ten years ago, the per capita income in the Pearl River Delta had already reached the level of that of moderately developed countries, and it is moving towards high-income phase. But the embarrassment is that in the eastern, western and northern parts of Guangdong Province, there are still large number of underdeveloped rural areas, and some places are even in extreme poverty, which distresses successive provincial governments. The government is determined to carry out large-scale "poverty alleviation" action, and vows to lift all peasants of impoverished areas out of poverty in three years, and promote common prosperity in these parts of Guangdong like the Pearl River Delta.

As the most populated, dynamic, and developed province that has been spearheading reform and opening up, recent practices in Guangdong are full of strength and sweetness. We go into it, and hope to find and record those breathtaking, touching and impressive stories of the development in Guangdong these years. Those people and those stories constitute a glaring part in the glittering development of the new era in Guangdong.

Through these stories, you can see diligence and endeavors of Guangdong people in the process of modernization. Through the perspective of Guangdong, you can see great efforts of Chinese people in realizing the China dream of the great rejuvenation of the Chinese nation.

总序

广东省位于中国南部，是中国最早实行改革开放的区域，也是目前中国最富庶的地区之一。中国的第三大河流珠江穿越广东省全境，由珠江冲积而成的珠江三角洲在经过近40年迅速发展后，已经成为中国最重要的城市群之一。香港特别行政区、澳门特别行政区与广东省毗邻，天然的地缘和一脉相承的人文情缘，构成了中国独有的粤港澳大湾区——一个世界级活跃的经济人文区域。

和中国其他地区一样，在经过长达近40年的高速发展之后，广东面临产业转型升级转变发展动能的重任，创新驱动成为推动此轮变革的重要抓手。广东省内有许多近年来快速成长起来的新型企业，比如华为、腾讯、有米科技，它们成为广东新经济发展的重要引擎。华为和腾讯，以及它们的"老板"任正非和马化腾，在中国几乎家喻户晓。我们试图走近这样的企业及其员工，找到广东创新驱动最前沿的发展"密码"。

广东自古以来是中国对外商贸最活跃的地区，广州是千年商都，是"海上丝绸之路"重要的节点城市。来自世界各地的外国人每天往来于广东省内各大城市，他们或旅游观光，或商务会议，或求学访友。在广州，每天大量来自欧美、东南亚、中东和非洲等地的外国人在这里做生意，他们把这里的服装、布匹、海产品、电器或者眼镜托运回国，外贸做得红红火火。在深圳经济特区口岸，进出香港和深圳的车辆、人流常常排成长龙。长年生活在这里的外国人，在生活习俗和文化上逐渐接受并慢慢融入广东，广东成为他们的"第二故乡"。与此同时，更多的数千万计的来自中国内地的普通劳工常年生活在广东尤其是珠江三角洲地区，他们在工厂里"打工"，凭借"打工"挣下的钱养家糊口，并试图实现自己的人生梦想。无论是外国人还是农民工，他们都是广东改革开放的实践者、推动者和见证者。我们近距离观察他们的工作和生活，记录他们的喜怒哀乐。

珠江三角洲地区早在10年前人均收入便已达到中等发达国家水平，正迈向高收入阶段。但令人尴尬的是，在广东省的东、西、北部仍有大片生活并不富裕的农村，一些地方甚至还处于贫困状态，这让广东省历届政府颇感头痛。政府下决心开展大规模的"扶贫"行动，并发誓要在3年后让所有贫困地区的农民摆脱贫困，力促粤东西北地区与珠江三角洲地区走向共同富裕。

作为人口最多、经济最活跃、总量最大、地处改革开放前沿的省份，广东近年的实践既具有力量又让人感到温馨。我们深入其中，希望通过我们去发现去记录，在广东发展这些年中，那些或动人心魄或充满温情或饱含人性的故事。那些人，那些事，终将构成广东新时期史诗般发展历程中炫目的一环。

通过这些故事，人们可以看见，在现代化进程中广东人的奋发图景；透过广东，可以看见中国人民为实现中华民族伟大复兴的中国梦的奋斗历程。

Contents

2

Contents

Contents

4

Contents

目 录

6

目　录

目　录

8

目 录

Poverty Alleviation of Guangdong's Poorest Villages: Eradicating Poverty in Limestone Mountain Regions

Leftovers in the Limestone Regions

In the movie *The Martian*, the hero Matt Monda, who is stuck on Mars alone and plants potatoes to live on, faces extremely difficult conditions. But at least the soil is fertile and he can harvest potatoes season after season. In Mengshan Village, however, with sufficient air, arable land and water are rare.

The limestone regions in Guangdong are 6,208 sq. km., accounting for 3.5% of the total area in the province and are mainly located in the northern and western part, with a few in the northeast. These regions share one thing in common: most of Guangdong's poorest villages are in these regions.

Mengshan is a small village located in Libu Town, Yangshan County of the northern Guangdong. It is a typical limestone region, with severe lack of soil and water, and an average attitude of over 500 meters. According to a survey conducted by the residency poverty—alleviation group when they first came to the village seven years ago, among all the 378 households were 127 poor families (437 people) and 69 families (171 people) with minimum allowances.

Why is Mengshan such a poor village? Let us first look at its natural environment conditions. In a mountain area, the most precious thing for farmers is arable land. However, all the land in Mengshan is scattered on the limestone hillside and, the small patches of land could hardly yield any economic benefits. Therefore, Mengshan villagers have to live toughly in the fragility of natural economy for the lack of mines, factories and power to change nature.

Many locals find it hard to describe their own farmland with exact words. The most classic self–mocking joke here is that on a rainy day, a farmer went up the mountain to cultivate land wearing a bamboo hat and when he arrived, the rain had stopped so he threw away the hat on the ground and started to turn the soil piece by piece. But after a day's exhausting work, he found that there was a missing patch of his land. He gave up looking for it and was about to pack things and went back home at dusk when he suddenly found the missing patch of land as he picked up the hat and discovered under it. This joke may sound exaggerated, but it shows exactly the embarrassing situation the villagers have been facing.

The scattering patches of land make it impossible to apply intensive farming in limestone areas. And even there are some plantable fields, the variety of crops is limited. High–value crops can barely be cultivated and only those like cassava and corn can grow in these fields.

The harsh environment also results in a drastic shortage of infrastructure construction. 285 out of the 440 units of paddy fields in Mengshan village are "fields on hill tops which depend on rains for irrigation" . Chen Jinsheng, head of the village committee, once said: "We can only harvest once a year and are not able to have irrigated agriculture. It's like watching the rain falls and having no way to keep and utilize it."

Long before the poverty alleviation group came, villagers had dreamed of digging several ponds to ease the lack of agricultural irrigation and drinking water. As early as the beginning of the 21st century, the locals have excavated a rill in the mountains which funnels the mountain spring water. Due to the financial limitations, the water was first funnelled into some 2—meter deep impounding reservoirs and when villagers used pipes to pump the water to their own house, there was little left.

Digging ponds and wells was the only way to solve the whole village's drinking water problem and the investment for this was up to RMB 200,000. But it was embarrassing that back then the village's income relied mainly on migrant workers' income and earnings from planting corps such as tea—oil trees and the average annual income per person could barely reached RMB 3,000, so it was totally impossible for them to spare money to build water conservancy project when they could hardly cover their daily expenses.

With global warming and stronger El Nino phenomenon, the World Bank has warned that 100 million people would become poor due to climate changes. And villagers from high—attitude limestone mountain areas in Guangdong are among this group.

Those living in limestone areas depend on Heaven for food, and once they encounter natural disasters like storms, snows, droughts and floods, they become even more vulnerable. Villagers with capability and skills have left the place for a better life. By 2013, no new house had been built in Mengshan Village and most of the local residents lived in the adobe house built between the 1930s and 1950s, with 1960s' slogans left on the exterior walls.

A Hometown
Migrants Cannot Go Back to

In 2016, China's "floating population" has reached 245,000,000. The phrase "floating population" refers to those who leave their domiciles of origin and live in other parts of China. In nearly 40 years after China's reform and opening up, the domestic floating population has been increasing, with a drastic growth after the 1990s, which went up from 6,570,000 in 1982 to 220,000,000 in 2010. It now accounts for 17% of the total population. In cities like Beijing, Shanghai and Guangzhou, the floating population occupies 40% of the local inhabitants. And most of them are young labor force moving from rural areas to cities.

The floating population go to big cities for better job opportunities and better lives. Seven years ago, most of the villages in the mountainous regions were bleak and desolate. Most of the villagers had left, leaving the elderly and children or those who had to take care of the elderly behind.

Has there been any changes in these villages in the past decade? The answer is yes. Actually some changes did take place in Mengshan village. But for the recent ten years, the only changes in most villagers' eyes lie in the construction of a gravel road and a two-storey committee office building. In 1997, the villagers raised about 20,000 yuan to construct a path toward bamboo forest and ponds. And the office building constructed in 1999 was sponsored by outworkers of Mengshan registry and poverty alleviation groups paid off the debts of the building construction.

Under the dual pressure of barren geographical conditions and gradually frequent natural disasters, some competent villagers chose to make a breakthrough for their lives by migrating and floating. But it didn't go smoothly. They lacked the skills and techniques to let them settle and develop in a new environment. They also faced a series of social problems such as children's education, employment and birth control planning due to the registry of residence.

In the 1990s, villagers made their first group leave to pull down buildings in Shunde, Foshan. However, most of the able-bodied men returned to the village because they earned little money and could not get accustomed to the lives outside the mountains. Xiong Huolan, a 67-year-old man took a different path. Instead of serving as a building-dismantling worker, he made his living on picking up rubbish in Lianzhou, a nearby county-level city. The work of Xiong is similar to that of those in Brazil slums. At that time China's main cities didn't set up a garbage classification system, and these junkmen took back the whole city's rubbish and picked out the recyclable materials to sell for the second time, which realized the full utilization of these materials. By virtue of his diligence and perseverance, Xiong got married when he was in his fifties. In Mengshan, the number of villagers like Xiong, who migrated to other places to make a living, has increased gradually in the first decade of the 21st century. In December 2000, the population in Mengshan was 1,944 and by the end of 2009 it had dropped to 1,823, apart from the few deceased people, the deducted population was mostly migrants.

But migration is not a once-for-all thing. For those migrants, they still face problems when they are making the transitions from countrymen to urbanites and it is not easy for them to have a durable and stable development because most of them have no specific skills.

In Lianma Village, Conghua, most of the young people have moved to cities or towns and just a few scattered households are living here.

Poverty Alleviation: Giving Hope to the Stay-at-home

The poverty of limestone mountain areas has long been a dilemma for Guangdong poverty alleviation work. For an area like Mengshan village, its deficiency in production resources and harsh living conditions dampens the effectiveness of government unremitting efforts in undertaking development−oriented anti−poverty measures.

From 1997, the local government did a series of work to help the poor in the area, such as distributing farming funds in order to help farmers invest enough money for production. But because of the difficulties in technology and sales, most of these farming funds became "living funds" and thus failed to reverse the impoverished living conditions.

How to vitalize local economy is really much learning. Mengshan village has a new look now: lush camellia trees are all over the mountains, sparkling white flowers give off light fragrance... Starting from the beginning of 2009, Guangdong Power Grid Qingyuan Administration of Power Supply and

Yangshan Supply and Marketing Cooperative worked hand in hand with Mengshan, Libu Town to adopt aiding measures. In three years' time, the 127 poverty-stricken households in the village have basically got rid of poverty. The locals did a thorough survey on the prospects of camellia and found that if 120 trees were planted in one unit of land and every unit produced 200 jin of tea oil, then they could got an overall income of 4,000 yuan at the average price of 20 yuan/jin. Currently there are around 400 units of land in Mengshan and each poor household could be allocated a plantation area from 2 to 5 units respectively.

It usually requires 3 to 5 years for a tea oil tree to produce fruits and about 10 years to reach the period of full productive years, with a steady fruit-harvest time for more than 80 years. Zhu Caiying, a 54 years old man is the only working labor in the family after his adult son developed mental disorder. His wife passed away due to cancer 8 years ago and they spent all the 100,000 savings for her treatment. Zhu said that: "I lent the 2 units of land to those who plant camellia trees and I'm also working for them. So as more fruits are harvested, I can earn more money in the future."

Financial Measures Taken to Help the Poorest Villages

The assistance group brought about production poverty elimination and also financial poverty relief. Yangshan was the first to put forward the idea of "poverty relief managers" and designated as "managers" village leaders or competent people who would work voluntarily to help the poor households. Residential village leaders looked for poor people who are diligent and have a strong desire to get rid of poverty, and helped them hand in hand. Yangshan Poverty Relief Office enlarged production by lending money to support "managers" and helped the poor through the efforts of those "managers".

What is more important is that Yangshan Poverty Relief Office underwrites 100,000 yuan for every village in the bank for a permission of 500,000 loans and has the "managers" act as underwriters. Supported by such financial innovation, Mengshan equips itself with several large–scale farming bases.

Villagers have long been facing the problem of fund shortage. To help Menghan raise enough funding, assistance group made a

On the morning of 30 June, 2016, the 2016 Guangdong Poverty Relief Day was launched in Guangzhou Zhudao Hotel. The charitable representatives from Guangdong enterprises and warm-hearted people attended the meeting and made donations. Guangdong Poverty Relief Outstanding Team (Project) raised banners to introduce the public charity projects.

creative move of setting up the village-level mutual help funds.

"Such funds can be view as 'village-level banks' ", introduced by Pan Zhiwei, director of Poverty Relief and Development Office. Village-level assistance funds are mainly raised by the government and nearly 400,000 yuan has been raised for Mengshan. The poor can lend 3,000 yuan with depositing any money in the bank.

"If working with a leading enterprise, we can apply loan that is no more than five-fold of the assistance fund from the agricultural bank." Pan elaborated this with an example, one poor household can apply 45,000 yuan loans from the agricultural bank if it can borrow 9,000 yuan at most.

Of course, the poor cannot casually borrow money from village assistance organizations unless they are underwritten by rich and influential families or more than three households. The "village–level banks" arouse villagers' interest in development. A villager called Jiang Siwen told us it cost 100,000 yuan to build a hog house to feed 300 pigs. Depending solely on himself, he could hardly raise so much money. But with the help of village–level mutual help funds, he finally made it to get tens of thousands of yuan. He said: "My ultimate goal is to have a hog house which can afford to feed housands of pigs."

Getting Rid of Poverty: Gaining Better Livelihood through Integral Moving

Considering the special geological features of limestone area and harsh living and production conditions, the locals in the mountainous areas in northern Guangdong have been alleviating poverty by effectively relocating people for the past decade. A relatively mature model for the locals is to move migrant population to a specific area and help them solve the problems of employment and children's education. It turns out that after the relocation, the residents have a higher income and mostly merges into the re-settlement communities.

Zhongchong is a village in Daqiao Town, Ruyuan Yao Autonomous County of Shaoguan, which is located deep in mountains and in the past, if one wants to get into the village, he would have to travel through highway to national road then to rural road and lanes.

It is one of the few villages in Guangdong that snow in winter and the mountains are covered in yellow when November comes every year. This place is a sleeping country compared with the

Pearl River Delta though it lies in the south of the Five Ridges.

However, things have changed. The Yao New Village on the hillside was built by the migrant Zhongchong villagers. Moving from mountains to the edge of the county, they now have a three−mile distance to the county and have a convenient transport because there is a newly−built round−the mountain−road at the gate of the village.

The relocation changes people's travel habits. For example, if the villager Zhao Tianxiang wants to go to the town before the 2010, he

In 9 August, 2011, the major parts of the first stage of Liwan-Lütian counterpart-assistance project have been completed and Su Zhijia dedicated the project. The project started from 18 May and was completed 20 days ahead of the planning date. The photo is the completion of the project's major parts. Photo taken by Gu Zhanxu.

would leave his house at dawn, walk for four hours on the mountain roads and rushed back home after quickly buying all the necessities in the county. This is because the route would get dangerous after it gets dark due to the narrow roads and steep cliffs.

After the reconstruction of Zhongchong village, children can study in the county's primary schools. The New Village is built in the style of Yao Minority and every villager has a two-storey building which has white walls, green bricks and red handrails, painted with Yao's ancient ornamentations. Leaving the mountains, villagers have more choices to make a living, such as engaging in agriculture or working in various industries.

Zhongchong started high mountain vegetable plantation from 2010 and now there are three bases: vegetable base, camellia base and yellow smoke base. High mountain vegetable has become a brand in Guangdong, and with eggplants, peppers and green beans transported to places like Guangzhou, Shenzhen, Dongguan, Daqiao Town (the place where Zhongchong is located) has become the vegetable basket in the Pearl River Delta.

Zhongchong is just an epitome of the integral moving in Guangdong poor mountainous areas. Dating back to the 1990s, Guangdong has begun the enormous work of migrant relocation. 100,000 Qingyuan Villagers have realized resettlement between 1994 and 1997 and another 300,000 Guangdong poor villagers made it from 2011 to 2016. After the relocation, the government would help build new dwellings and matching facilities and the farmers thus directly move from the places with harsh natural environment to relatively advanced regions and enjoy the public services there.

There are eight projects in the latest Guangdong Poverty Relief policies, one of which is to consolidate the results of relocation by improving living conditions in resettlement areas and support the building of infrastructure in resettlement regions and the ecological restoration of out—migration areas; to arrange "staying with relatives and friends" migration for those scattered poor households who do not have living and production conditions; and to transform the minority poor people with labor capacity who are not willing to relocate into ecological protection staff such as forest rangers by applying eco—compensation mechanism.

Educational Poverty Alleviation: Enhancing Education Level before Implementing Poverty Alleviation

"The Sahara Desert" in Leizhou

Leizhou Peninsula, located in the southernmost point of China, borders on the Beibu Gulf in the west, the South China Sea in the east and is separated by the 18—sea—mile Qiongzhou Strait with Hainan Island to the south. About 5,000 to 6,000 years ago, there were ready human beings on this red earth and it was brought into Huaxia (ancient China) in the Qin dynasty and was the location of the ancient Hepu county governance. Leizhou Peninsula was also an important base for foreign trade in Han dynasty and the original port of "Maritime Silk Road" . It was after the Tang dynasty that the governors had the plan of "moving Cantonese to Hezhou" (Hezhou was later changed into Leizhou in the Tang Zhenguan Eighth Year). The southward migration increased year by year after the Song dynasty, which stepped up the development speed of Leizhou Peninsula. The Peninsula people have created various unique intangible cultures in the past hundreds of thousands of years. Leizhou song, performed in the Peninsula's distinct dialect Leiyu, is the country's intangible cultural heritage. And there are great differences between the dialect of Leizhou and those in other parts of Guangdong, especially the relatively richer Pearl River Delta area.

Located in Leizhou Peninsula, Dongtang village has a strange phenomenon: ever since the reform and opening up, no matter how many young labor leave the place to work elsewhere, they would all return to the province—known poor village in the end because they find themselves unsecure to work in places outside their hometown.

According to a survey made in 2010, there were 908 households, 3,957 people in Dongtang, and 2,021 people among 468 households were living under the poverty line, making a poverty rate of over 51%. And as it was said by the World Bank that China's overall poverty rate was around 53%, we could tell the living standards in Dongtang still stood at the level of the 1980s.

Wang Nan has been working as the village secretary for 13 years on this barren land. It was not until 2010 that he made a farewell to cottage room and moved into red brick house with the help of his two brothers.

Why was poverty alive all the time in this small village? And how did poverty alleviation take effect there?

It is necessary to first illustrate the environment in Leizhou by comparing it with the Sahara Desert. The Sahara Desert is located in the north of Africa, stretching from the Mediterranean in the north to the Sudan Prairie in the south. The desert was formed about 250,000,000 years ago and is the second largest desert and the largest gravel desert in the world. Located in the northern Africa, it is regarded as one of the most unsuitable places for biological existence. Leizhou Peninsula is often called by people as the "Sahara Desert" in Leizhou.

The natural environment in Dongtang can be described as "harsh". The lands are barren and suffer from severe desertification. In rainy seasons, the sea wind brings plentiful rainfall and leaves water stored in the fields, which cannot be emptied for half a year but in some dry months, villagers have to watch the seedlings die.

Since the 21st century, China has invested much capital in agriculture and the purchasing prices for grains have gone up gradually, with the minimum rice price reaching 1 yuan/jin in Guangdong. However, such progress seems to make no benefits to Dongtang villagers, and even in good years they can only feed themselves with the food planted. In fact, villagers are relying on the Heaven rather than fields for food because even in the best years, they can only harvest up to 500 units of food. But in other regions, villagers can harvest more than thousands of units of food with the application of mechanized planting. However, as most people in Dongtang only attend primary or secondary schools, many of them "haven't heard about" scientific farming. In Dongtang, mechanized planting is an untrodden area and in the eyes of the under-educated villagers, new equipment such as tractors and fertilizers are troublesome things.

Before the year 2010, Li Xuegui was utterly destitute and there was no calendar, no clocks in his house. Being an illiterate, Li has been living a life of doing farming work with neighbors in the morning and coming back home at night for many years. In order to increase production with the limited lands, Li had to plant sweet potatoes once she had reaped the rice. Some technicians had told the villagers how to raise yields by scientific farming, but she and her neighbors could not remember and perform it.

At weekends, Li's children had to go back home and do farm work on the fields, and they needed to live in their neighbor's house since there was no vacant beds for them. The family devoted all their efforts to planting and preserving their land because they fed themselves with it and in good years, they might have a good harvest. Unfortunately, almost no families could have left food for sale. Some villagers have tried to plant peanuts or peppers but they just "had passion rather than techniques" and lost money in spite of a year's hard work.

An Outer World
that Cannot Be Fitted into

In the 1990s, millions of workers swarmed into the Pearl River Delta, a paradise filled with job opportunities.

Dongtang villagers were among the migrant workers. The swirling wheels took those with dreams of making money and supporting families to the outer world. However, luck seemed to escape them—no one was heard of making money outside and the migrant workers soon went back to the village.

Over a decade has passed, villagers said nothing had changed but the dirt road leading to the village had been covered with cement.

In the house of Zhengxin, the red bricks bought four years ago were still piled at the corner and already covered with moss. In 2006, the cottage Zheng lived in for several decades were worn down. When it rained outside, there would be a flood in the room. After a heavy rain this year, the cottage underwent a disaster and almost half of it collapsed.

It was in exactly the same year that Zheng Xin's 22-year-old son went to work in Guangdong under the recommendation of friends after graduating from junior high school. The family decided to build a new house considering there would be financial support since their eldest son went to big cities to work. They quickly spent all the 20,000 yuan lent from relatives while their son could hardly feed himself in Guangzhou. The young people, with no understanding of mandarin or specific skills, had to live on picking up rubbish with fellow villagers. The family's dream of building a house was gone and so did their old cottage. Under desperation, they moved to the nearby forest and set up two "wooden tents" with branches. The smaller one was for Zhao Xin's mother and his wife and he lived in the bigger one. Having been working for four years, Zheng Xin's eldest son could only earn a monthly wage of 800 yuan. In his calls with his grandmother, the boy told her he wanted to go back home and do farm work because the outer world was too harsh.

The middle-aged in the village once had the similar experience as Zheng's eldest son. They went to work in the Pearl River Delta or neighboring provinces and came back after at most three years. The fundamental cause for this phenomenon is that Dongtang villagers speak "Leizhou Mandarin" and the heavy accent is hard to be understood. As a result, their promotion is hindered by ineffective communication.

The mouthful of "Leizhou mandarin" originates from Dongtang primary school. On the classes before 2010, the teacher was teaching children Pinyin in mandarin by stressing every single syllable. But as he turned around and shouted "Be quite!" to the students, the accent changed into Leizhou dialect. At that time, both the 301 student and all the teachers were local residents and with less than 1/20 households owning a television and almost none knowing about the Internet, they were helplessly shunned from the outer world.

Most of the teachers in Leizhou stay at the school to teach once they graduated from the sixth grade and get diplomas for refresher courses after years of teaching, so they have missed the prime time to learn mandarin. As a result, "Leizhou mandarin" is handed down from generation to generation. On the surface, however, the rate for primary school students entering secondary school is 100%. As most rural children go to school at an older age and it is "quite common for them to enter primary school at eight", most of the junior school starters in Dongtang are over 16 years old.

The old junior graduates with strong Leizhou accent repeat the path of their father's generation. The difficulties in reality cannot lessen their eagerness for entering the outer world. Throng of Dongtang villagers come back to their hometown with tears in their eyes after a year or two of tough lives in the big cities. They take over the hoes from their father's hands, marry and raise children, and end their lives in poverty and mediocrity.

Made in China 2025 Initiative and Educational Poverty Alleviation

The conception of "Made in China 2025" was first put forward in December, 2014. Four months later, on 5 March, 2015, Premier Li Keqiang came up with the grand strategy when he was making a report on government work on NPC and CPPCC. The strategy is the program of action for the first decade of Chinese government's strategy of building a powerful manufacturing country. The first step is to shift China from a big manufacturing country to a strong one by 2025. The second one is to make China able to compete with developed manufacturing powers by 2035. The third one is to transform China into a leading manufacturing power by 2049.

Qualified professionals are indispensable to complete such an upgrading task of manufacturing industry as "Made in China 2025". As urbanization advances, the large number of migrant workers in Guangdong has the potential of becoming qualified industrial workers. High quality workers are in great demand in the Pearl River Delta. However, poverty prevents those from mountainous areas from learning technical knowledge and getting systematic training. The status quo of education in Dongtang village also reveals the problems facing Guangdong's poverty alleviation work: insufficient input for educational infrastructure, unbalanced allocation of faculty and uncertain prospects for graduates.

For those poor households and their children, it is not a long—run plan to relieve their poverty by simply giving them clothes, food and shelters. To relieve the poor we first need to enhance the educational levels. Actually, all the residents in the mountains know that they need to leave their hometown so as to become rich and that they have to equip themselves with knowledge before leaving. To guarantee the effect of poverty alleviation on "individual" , good mandarin skills and enhanced cultural qualities are the prerequisites.

In December 2009, Shenzhen Pingshan New Area became assistance partners with the four villages in Dongli Town, including Dongtang village. It was acknowledged that professional skills could not be improved if people have low mandarin levels. For the 198 people with work capability in the poor households of Dongtang, Pingshan New Area arranged free technical skill training tours under the principle of "one trained, one employed, one alleviated from poverty" . The area also organized purposefully villagers to work there and master techniques and accumulate experience to make preparation for future returning to the village and achieving integral poverty alleviation.

At the same time, the Dongtang Primary School, standing at the side of the village road, had taken on a new appearance. A reinforced concrete public toilet was built in the southwest of the school with a 33,600 yuan fund from Pingshan New Area. A garbage pool, constructed over the same period, thoroughly settled the 300 teachers' and students' difficulty in using toilet and remarkably improved the school's environment.

Outside the village, some strangers encounter several kids riding bikes and playing around. They think those children can not understand mandarin, just like the adults they meet along the road. To their surprise, one boy suddenly comes near and asks in mandarin: "Where are you going?"

Eliminating Ignorance before Combating Poverty

On 16 October, 2015, Yang Guoqiang, founder of Country Garden Co., Ltd in Shunde, was awarded "China's Poverty Elimination Prize" (Innovation Prize) on the Alleviation and Development High-level Forum. He launched the mutual assistance model of "government and society" in education area. Yang Guoqiang and his daughter have donated over 1.3 billion yuan to Guangdong's poverty alleviation project since 2010. The 800 million donated before had been used for six projects: the green industry poverty relief in Qingyuan, Zhaoqing and Guangzhou, the poverty alleviation in Huaiji county, the poverty alleviation in Timian town, technique and skill trainings in villages, establishment of Guangdong Country Garden Professional School and targeted poverty alleviation.

Born in a poor farmer family in Shunde, Guangdong, Yang hardly wore shoes before he was seventeen. He could never forget that the government exempted his tuition fees of 7 yuan per semester and gave him 2 yuan as grant to let him finish the high school course otherwise he had to drop out of school due to poverty. He deeply felt the positive influence of education upon thoroughly eliminating poverty. Thus, he stepped onto the road of educational poverty elimination after becoming a successful entrepreneur.

After all these years, when Yang Guoqiang recollected his past years of striving, he believed he was driven by the desire for knowledge. To further explain this point, Yang gave us an example: when he and his cousin, now the Chief Financial Officer of Country Garden, received the 2 yuan allowance and exemption of tuition fees, they went to buy a lot of books with the money they had.

In 1997, Yang donated one million yuan and anonymously set up the "Zhongming Scholarship" to support poverty-stricken college students and 8,000 students have benefited from the scholarship in the past 18 years. Yang also established the Guohua Memorial Secondary School with an input of 260 million yuan in 2002, which enrolled extraordinary students from poor families and offered them grant till they got bachelor's, master's or even doctor's degrees. Eleven years later, Yang invested 350 million yuan in starting the Guangdong Country Garden Professional School, where students would be exempted from all expenses and be given subsidies. The school is currently a typical educational poverty alleviation project in Guangdong. Now it has an enrollment of 672 poor students. And after two years of student recruitment, most of the students are Cantonese.

In 2012, Yang Guoqing developed another way of educational poverty alleviation in Shuitou Town, Fogang County, Qingyuan. He started a "technique and skill training project in villages" by moving the professional classrooms to villages. The project targeted the working-age population between 16 and 60 years old, offering them free skill training and helping the trainees to get jobs by contacting personnel companies and employing units. For the last three years, the project have trained 16,469 people, with 8,150 obtaining 9 kinds of job qualification certificates for forklift drivers, electricians, nurses and so on and 3,828 working in the cities under recommendation.

Yang believes, on the one hand, that the college need to systematically cultivate labourers with high quality and proficient skills and on the other hand, that people's biased attitudes towards vocational schools should be changed as more high–level employment taking place among those who attend such schools.

Yang's ideas were verified to be true according to a survey made by the Ministry of Human Resources and Social Security. It was said

Implement the principle of eliminating ignorance before combating poverty. Volunteers of poverty elimination are building mobile library for children in mountainous areas with donated books.

that among the 225,000,000 second–industry working population, only 119,000,000 were skilled craftsmen. Up to over 400 million working force was needed for senior mechanic in manufacturing industry alone and the severe conflict between the demand and supply of skilled craftsmen hindered the advancement of corporation technological upgrade. Yang Guoqiang, as a member of the national committee of CPPCC, handed in "A Proposal for Encouraging and Instructing Private Enterprises to Actively Join in Educational Poverty Alleviation" on the 2015 CPPCC. Emphasizing professional educational poverty alleviation has gained support from institutions on the national level. The State Council has issued a regulation which set up clear goals for establishing the modern professional education system.

Although educational alleviation requires heavy input, troublesome process and long period of time and is hard to persevere, it has a notable effect in realizing "cultivate one person, relieve one household from poverty" policy and thoroughly preventing poverty from being handed down to next generations. Undoubtedly, it can actualize a win–win relationship among individuals, families and society. In Yang's 18 years of educational poverty alleviation, around 40,000 people have got rid of poverty. Yang said: "The wealth I gained is the thing I hold in custody for society, so it's natural to help others when I'm capable. I'm just performing my responsibility. I always feel the most important thing in a man is his qualities and educational poverty alleviation is 'teaching a man how to fish'."

Medical Poverty Alleviation: Eliminating the Root of Poverty for 600,000 People

Illness Hinders
the Steps towards Wealth

Health and sanitation holds a crucial position in relieving or even eliminating poverty. Margaret Chan Fung Fu−chun, secretary−general of the World Health Organization, pointed out in her speech on the 2015 Poverty Alleviation and Development Forum that sanitation, health and poverty were closely interrelated. Poverty will influence people's health and things such as poor, unhealthy, unsanitary environment, lack of nutrition and misuse of medication and tobaccos will challenge one's spiritual and physical health. It is evident that people with better body can get rid of poverty more easily.

In the 1.765 million relatively poor population in Guangdong, the proportion of people who suffer from poverty due to illness is up to 36.2%. It means that illness has become the biggest stumbling block on the way of Guangdong's effort in getting rid of poverty for those in mountainous areas. One person falls sick, the family falls apart. So how to offer sufficient medical treatment to farmers is a major obstacle for Guangdong's poverty relief work.

In southern Guangdong, villagers from Xikou, Meizhou could hardly feed the whole family with the four pieces of land per person. As there is a severe unbalance between demand and supply, the only solution is to "find work outside the mountains". Xikou villagers have long known this is the way out of poverty, but not all of them can leave their hometown and work in the counties or travel further to the Pearl River Delta. In some households, the family members suffer from diseases and lose labor capability. As a result, they don't have affluent workforce for the outer world and the families are thus dragged back from their way of accumulating wealth by the cirrus-like illness.

Diseases sweep over these families, leaving only one or two solitary members who are capable to work. Xikou village is located in the south of Qingxi town, Dapu county, Meizhou. Prior to the year 2010, the village had a population of 1,748 and a total of 181 poor households and 726 poor people earned an annual income of less than 1,500 yuan. There were 242 units of paddy fields, and most people had to work as migrant workers since each one could be allocated with only 4 pieces of land.

Having worked outside for 30 years, Liu Changxi returned to Xikou with almost nothing, and the adobe house aside of the 332 Provincial Road was all he had. He has been striving to change his destiny for half of his life, only to find himself defeated by illness.

Liu Changxi was among the group of the earliest migrant workers in the local area after the reform and opening up. In 1997, Liu left his home, but the elementary school graduate could only travel around and work with low wages because he failed to enter the state-owned mining factory. Under someone's recommendation, Liu was hired by a local in Longmen county to take care of the commercial crop on the mountains. Ten years later, Liu married a woman 15 years younger than him in his fifties, who was a widow with epilepsy.

Marriage, while bringing Liu a sense of belonging, doomed his improving life. His wife suffered a lot from the illness and Liu travelled everywhere to find medical treatment for her. "New rural cooperative medical system" hasn't been popularized at the beginning of the 1990s, and Liu was suffocated by the dual burden of medical fees and travelling expenses.

In 2010, the 76-year-old Liu died in his combat with poverty and illness and his path was followed by the 41-year-old Ding Ruihui. After his wife's death in 2006, Ding abandoned his identity as a rural migrant worker and took up farm work in order to take care of his elderly parents and three young daughters. Before his wife passed away, their life was just better off and they built two brick houses in the village, but Ding owed a 40,000 yuan debt to pay for his wife's treatment and he couldn't pay it off after four years of his wife's death.

Ding had a family of six people and owned only three pieces of land. He had to work part time in Chayang and Qingxi town after busy seasons. Financing his parents' medical treatment and his daughter's living expenses in secondary school with an unstable income, Ding scarcely had extra money at hand.

Xikou is just an epitome of the poverty-stricken people caused who suffer from illness. Some migrant workers do succeed in getting rid of poverty, but others could hardly earn a good salary because they are under-educated. Li Qingxiang, cadre of poverty-relief work, believes that since currently most young workers from the poor mountainous areas only graduate from secondary school and complete the basic compulsory education, they could only do the bottom layer jobs when they're in the outside world.

Illness-related poverty has mainly two causes. On the one hand, farmers could not afford the medical expenses due to vulnerable economic base. On the other hand, illness deprives the family members of their labor capability and leads to family's living standards falling under poverty line when there is only one grown—man supporting the whole family.

Li Qingxiang said: "Some family members lose their labor capability or even die when they catch certain diseases, which in the end leads to the family's worsening situation, and such households account for the majority of poor families. And a major difficulty for the anti—poverty project is the poverty—returning phenomenon due to illness.

In the end all the reasons for poverty make up one clue: farmers migrant work in other places because they can't make a fortune through traditional farming due to insufficient lands—migrant workers have a low wage and live in poverty for lack of cultural knowledge—and some families have to bear the burden of expenses for medical treatment or lose working labor (infected with disease or die), and thus become the poorest groups of people.

The Ups and Downs
in Rural Medical Care

Seven years ago, for the 300 people production team Liu Changxi worked in, only one clinic was equipped to take care of them. Back then, the status quo of the medical conditions in poverty−stricken mountainous areas was that most primary physicians were from junior colleges or technical secondary schools, so it would be impossible for them to cure all kinds of illness.

Tu Qizhi, dean of a health−center, felt quite helpless when speaking of the embarrassing situations in the past seven or eight years as they didn't have enough health resources. At that time, he only had a staff team of 10 doctors and three nurses.

Besides a shortage of manpower, the health center was also poorly−equipped, with a black and white ultrasound machine being the most advanced facility. And when the elderly doctors retired, successors could not be found. Tu used to ask for personnel from Dapu Sanitary Bureau, but he knew the possibility of ever finding one was rare. He explained it was because the low salary offered by them was of little attraction.

Dean Tu then had a monthly wage of about 1,500 yuan, and the doctors graduated from junior colleges and technical secondary schools earned 700 yuan and 600 yuan respectively.

With a widening gap between the wages of county health centers and urban hospitals, many experienced doctors flock to cities and fewer people go to clinics to treat their illness.

As an elementary healthcare worker, Tu empathizes farmers' difficulty in seeing a doctor.

Currently, China's basic healthcare insurance is mainly divided into three categories: working people healthcare insurance, medical insurance for urban residents and new rural cooperative medical system (NCMS). Among these, medical insurance for urban residents are paid by government finance and residents themselves and managed by the Bureau of Human Resources and Social Security while the NCMS is paid by government and farmers and managed by the Bureau of Health and Family Planning.

In the 1970s, China's rural cooperative medical service system, county–countryside–village medical care system in rural areas and barefoot doctors were considered as the "three magic weapons" for solving the lack of doctors and medication in villages and protecting public's health. The rural cooperative model was highly commended by the World Health Organization and the World Bank as "the model of largest health benefits with least input" and was introduced to the developing countries. Cooperative medical service was written into the Constitution of PRC in 1978 and prior to the reform of rural production responsibility regulations in agriculture, the coverage of rural medical service had been up to 80% to 90%.

After the 1980s, villages initiated the household contract responsibility system. People's commune was abolished, production team disassembled, leading to a quick shrink of rural collective economy. This was soon followed by the disintegration of cooperative medical service system. As most village clinics and cooperative medical service stations became the private clinic of country doctors, the phenomenon of farmers' lack of doctors and medication reappeared. According to a survey, the cooperative medical service coverage dropped dramatically from 68.8% in 1980 to below 20% in 1983. It was said by the 1985's statistics that the villages implementing cooperative medical service went straight down from 90% to 5%. The Chinese government have again attempted to reconstruct the rural cooperative system by carrying out "privately run under state ownership and voluntary participation" in the 1990s, but they failed to reach the expected desire for recovery and construction as the system designed didn't clearly state the government's entity responsibility in securing the society. One set of data can be used to illustrate the embarrassing situation of rural cooperative medical service: while in 1979 the national finance health care costs granted 100 million yuan to the cooperative system, the figure dropped to 35 million in 1992, which only accounted for 0.36% of the total health care costs.

At the beginning of this century, with an increasingly unbalanced development in urban and rural areas, China restarted the construction of rural cooperative medical service system in October 2002 and renamed it as a new system. The new rural cooperative system adopted a financing mechanism of individual payment, collective support and government funding. The cooperative medical service funding was mainly used to subsidize farmers' large−sum or hospitalized medical bills, forbidding overspending or excessive balance. The updated NCMS, besides targeting at outpatient and hospitalization services, also includes the insurance for serious illness. Take Guangzhou as an example, nowadays rural residents only have to pay 100 yuan/year for the system, then they can get a grant of 340 yuan/year from local governments, a reimbursement limit of 50% and 70% for outpatient and hospitalization services. If they catch some serious illness, they can enjoy an over 50% reimbursement for the self-paid expenses. The maximum limit is 150,000 yuan/year.

At the beginning of 2016, Guangdong province actualized the integration of rural and urban medical care insurance systems. After this, the scales and medication catalogues of local fixed medical care institutions have witnessed an evident enlargement. Now urban and rural residents use the same basic medicine insurance catalogue, and the reimbursable medication categories for farmers have increased.

Medical Poverty Alleviation: A "One Package Service" to Relieve Poverty

Besides the enhancement of new rural cooperative medical system, Guangdong is also using new systems and technologies to solve the problems in medical poverty alleviation.

Liannan is a poverty–stricken region in Guangdong province and there are considerable gaps between Liannan's and the average provincial medical and health standards. Three big hospitals were once located here, but due to the limitations in medical technologies and environment, an estimated rate of 40% of locals would go to the neighboring Lizhou or Lianshan to see doctors. How to have the patients go to local hospitals to see doctors?

Officials in Guangdong College of Pharmacy suggest that the college's assistance to Liannan People's Hospital is out of the accountability of public welfare and social responsibility rather than commercial purposes. After the collocation, the hospital adopted a management mode of de–administrative corporate representative, and set up a decision–making level board and a supervisory committee supervising the former's exercise of power.

All the positions in the hospital were de—administrated and rankings were removed, with leading groups appointed by the board. The management team and technical experts sent by the Guangdong College of Pharmacy also greatly enhanced the standards of Liannan Hospital.

Besides the new rural cooperative medical system and effective medical resources allocation, new technologies also put forward solutions to the problems of medical poverty alleviation. The 91—year—old Liang Bao had a stroke six years ago and was half—paralyzed, he could only move around in his just over 10 square meters room and was unable to take a sunbath in front of his house, not to mention going to see a doctor. On 16 October, 2016, a Yangshan family doctor team launched by Yanshan Medical Group of Guangdong No.2 People's Hospital and Guangdong Network Hospital

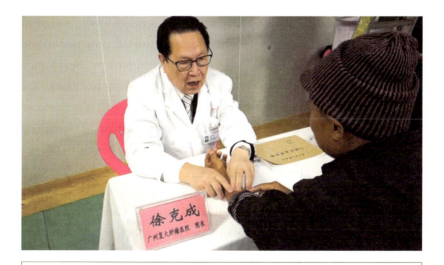

Xu Kecheng, a renowned doctor, is carrying out a free clinic to relieve regional poverty. Free clinic in medical poverty alleviation campaigns let the renowned doctors go to grassroot levels to provide high quality medical services for local residents.

arrived at the Fan village (Yangshan county, Qingyuan) Liao Bao lived and signed a contract with him to provide him with free targeted treatment. It was a new welfare offered by provincial No.2 People's Hospital of Yangshan Hospital Group.

The data released by Guangdong Poverty Alleviation Office in August 2016 showed that the major three reasons causing poverty among the relatively poor households in the province were illness (36.2%), lack of labor (23.3%) and disability (19.9%). Yangshan is just an epitome of poor mountainous regions. There are 159 villages in Yanghshan, and Zhou Qiru, the Dean of Guangdong Network Hospital, and his staff screened out over 2,000 illness—related poor households by traveling from villages to villages.

In order to have good quality medical resources come to the grassroots and improve country's medical and health care services levels, Yangshan Medical Group of Guangdong No.2 People's Hospital proposed to use "internet and public health care" to carry out medical poverty alleviation.

Experts find that, in Yangshan, there are many residents like Liang Bao, who cannot travel far to see doctors and must be provided with door—to—door service. The online and offline healthcare management team from the Guangdong Network Hospital have started a "one package" service for these people. The family doctor team is composed of village doctors, doctors from township health centers and the Guangdong Network Hospital and party members and experts from Yangshan Medical Group of Guangdong No.2 People's Hospital. After signing an agreement, doctors will complete the establishment of health profiles for these households and track and update the profiles on time. Besides, they will also provide some individualistic preferential services such as tracking the diseases of the elderly, the young and women, serious and chronic diseases and sharing provincial, prefectural, town and village—level medical resources.

The over 2,000 "illness—caused poverty" households in Yangshan will all sign agreements with the family doctor team. Within two years, the sicken members in these families will get free and concise treatment and get health management, which aims at improving their living standards fundamentally and let them get rid of poverty.

Let us turn back to the story of Liu Changxi. Now he has joined the new rural cooperative medical system and with the coverage of serious illness insurance, the reimbursement proportion for his wife's disease has drastically increased and the plight of his family has relieved a lot. In the meantime, as the medical power comes down to villages, two community doctors who have received professional training have arrived at the production brigade Liu Changxi's in. As a result, he needn't go to the town dozens of miles away to see doctors.

Establishing Transportation System to Relieve Poverty: Building a Good Road for Villages—A Way Out and A Way to Survive

Smooth Artery
but Blocked Blood Capillary

Ever since China's reform and opening up, farmers have learned many lessons on their way to wealth, and the most notable one is "If you want to be rich, build a road first. And road is the criteria of whether a region is rich or not". From this, we can tell the great importance of village roads in China's economic development. Transportation is crucial for economic growth and keeping village roads open is a key for rural economic development.

Guangdong, as the one of the earliest provinces launching reform and opening up, has been playing a leading role in the construction of infrastructure such as transportation. By the end of 2015, the traffic mileage of Guangdong highway has reached 7,018 miles, being the first province in China that outnumbers 7,000 miles. Guangdong has realized the goal of "making every county connected to highways", and has 17 routes leading out of the province and over three land routes connecting to the neighboring provinces. While the eastern, western and northern parts of Guangdong have an evidently improved highway network and a transport mileage of 3,282 miles, an extensive and balanced highway backbone network is basically taking into shape. The figures show the great investment and achievement of Guangdong's road construction. However, such constructions mostly take place in highly—developed areas such as the Pearl River Delta, and for the mountainous areas in the eastern, western and northern parts of Guangdong, there is still a lot that needs to be done for transportation infrastructure construction.

Located in Heyuan, Yangmei village used to be a place that was filled with over—aged youth who couldn't find wives due to the blocking traffic. "Even though the boys have good looks, that's useless for helping them get married." When asked about the cause of poverty, all the villagers pointed out it was because of "the worn—out roads" .

The difficulty in getting out of the village was the residents' deepest memories. In earlier years, it took Yangmei villagers a long time to arrive at Heyuan. Leaving at 7.30 in the morning, villagers had to travel on the mountain road for two hours, walked out of the eastern mountain to arrive at Xichang Harbor, took a ferry—boat and reached Heyuan at 12.30 at noon. If they failed to settle their affairs in the afternoon, they had to stay at a hotel and leave the other day.

Villagers Are Longing for Good Roads

Zhan Shiyuan once planted dozens of units of fruit trees in 2001, but he told us: "Due to the worn–out mountain road, the buyers don't want to come to the village and when they do come, they would demand a lower price. For example, one could spend a few dimes to buy the goods that are sold at 1 yuan outside." Almost all villagers lose money for their investment because of the inconvenient transportation. No matter for vegetables or fruit, the delivery truck would be waiting outside the mountains, and villagers have to carry the goods on a seven miles journey eastward. Yangmei village has a broken gun carrier retired from the troop and it is the only vehicle to deliver goods through the mud roads. The villagers have to spend 150–200 yuan for every delivery, and this covers cost of labor, truck–rental fees and expenses for wait times.

In 2008, a farmer from Heshikeng village, Xichang Town successfully cultivated glossy ganoderma in the reservoir area and thus earned a considerable income. Then the plantation of glossy ganoderma was popularized all over the town and Dongyuan county even named Xichang as "glossy ganoderma specialized town" . The cultivation of glossy ganoderma seemed to overnight become the magic weapon for Yangmei villagers to get rid of poverty. In the first year, the planters earn thousands of yuan. Other villagers rushed forward the next year and the dozens of growers had 12 units of plantation altogether. In 2009, villager Li Yamin used six Dongfeng trucks to deliver wood, spent 6,000 yuan on seedlings and cultivated over 2,500 jins of glossy ganoderma.

However, Yangmei villagers were painful to learn that the seedlings in the wooden stakes were dead by May and piles of wood, steamed and inserted with seedlings, could only be used to make fire. The villagers said: "We still haven't figured out the causes by now. Some say the woods were infected, but no experts would come here and give us instructions."

Through their efforts, the 10.5-mile country road leading to the town to the east side of the village was finally open to traffic in 2007. But for the 7-mile economic way in the west, the villagers failed to get project approvals after several attempts. The researchers of the National Leading Group of Poverty Alleviation and Development discovered from the survey of eastern provinces' poverty relief work that the infrastructure construction in Guangdong poor areas was highly backward, which failed to fit with industrial development and there was still a lot of heavy work unfinished for improving poverty-stricken people's living standards.

It was not until 2012 that Yangmei village got approved for the construction of the economic road in the west side with the help of poverty alleviation institutions. The village had the road open to traffic by the end of that year with the 240 million funding.

A Good Road Is A Way Out and A Way to Survive

Sishui is an assisted village in the last round's (2013—2015) poverty alleviation campaign household—and individual—targeted and has got rid of poverty by now. Wang Manxiu, provincial NPC member, party branch secretary and director of village committee of Sishui, concluded from the experience of poverty alleviation work that country roads had to be built in order to help poor villagers accumulate wealth. Sishui villagers mainly planted vegetables and trees, but the goods could only rot in the fields because there were no roads for dealers and delivery. Many poor villages face the same circumstances as Sishui: they are not scarce in resources or industries, but they couldn't sell their good quality agricultural products or develop and promote tourism resources because of inaccessible transportation. The farmers are living a worsening life as natural organic food rot in the lands and beautiful natural sceneries are hidden behind mountains since farmers can't go out and enterprises can't get in.

In order to propel rural economic development, the locals

The photo is a scene of the mutual-assistance poverty alleviation and development project bewteen Dongyong Town, Fanyu District and Paitan Town. On 21 June, 2016, in Chinese Yam Horizontal Planting Technology Agricultural Demonstration Base, a farmer is pruning branches for a well-grown Chinese yam. Now, Guangzhou is financing eight poor counties to get rid of poverty by building public facilities and establishing new economic industries. (Photo taken by Shao Quanda)

need to increase investment in country road construction, enhance environment for transportation and smooth the way for the adaptation of rural industrial structure and commodity circulation to promote farmers' earnings.

If Guangdong wants to lead in establishing a moderately prosperous society in 2018, poverty alleviation is a key battle for it to win. "Implementing

Infrastructure Construction Poverty Alleviation Project" is clearly stated as one of the eight Guangdong's poverty alleviation projects. The project aims at not only building roads, but also establishing an effectively interconnected transportation system. Besides offering paths for people to travel through, these roads are also expected to develop industries, vitalize resources, increase incomes for the poor villages.

On the basis of opening highways in every county, Guangdong Provincial Transportation Bureau has drawn up a plan of further enhancing highway network in poor regions and establishing more roads leading to these regions by 2018. The project, focusing on reconstructing county roads, tends to improve the country road construction in poor areas.

The village He Guifang (member of the National People's Congress, party branch secretary and director of village committee of Shanlian village) comes from used to be called as the "Siberia" of Liannan because it had a backward transportation system, blocked information source and laggard development. Over the years, under He's advocation, the roads have been connected, electricity are on, development speeds up and villagers' living standards improve. He believes that the key for Guangdong's improving the production and living standards in poor mountainous areas lies in making up the shortage in rural development. He Youlin, member of the National People's Congress, former principal of Zhongshan Memorial Secondary School, said that: "It's essential to build good roads for villages. For villagers, a good road is not only a way out, but also a way to survive."

Financial Poverty Alleviation: Stepping up the Way of Overcoming Poverty

Lack of Funding in Agriculture: A Financial Deficit in Spring Ploughing

Speaking of the poverty–stricken areas in Guangdong, the first that comes to people's minds is those in the eastern, western and northern parts of Guangdong. However, poverty also exists in the Pearl River Delta. Jinkeng village is one example. Located in Dongcheng Town in Jiangmen Wuyi areas, the village has an area of 104,000 square kilometers and in its five natural villages, there are 471 households and a total population of 1,499. The villagers make their living mainly on planting rice with low added value. Villagers and the village committee have an average annual income of 3,100. Besides starting business abroad, some villagers also work in Enping, Jiangmen, Zhongshan and Guangzhou.

Lack of funding is one of the major issues restricting the agricultural development in Jinkeng.

In 1995, a banking crisis outbroke in Enping as a result of attracting deposits by high interests. The banks went bankrupt one by one and there was a recession in the development of local financial institutions for more than a decade. The local commercial banks cut down dramatically its service network stations, coming down from 266 before the financial crisis to 43 now.

In rural areas, as Enping's urban and rural cooperatives have been canceled, financial services could only depend on postal savings banks since other financial institutions either don't have agricultural financial services or "only permit deposits but don't offer loans". According to statistics, the local loan balance was only 480,000 yuan by the end of 2007, accounting for barely 0.03% of the agricultural loans in Jiangmen areas.

Jinkeng is just an epitome of the poor villages in Guangdong. Since 1998, the support for issues of agriculture, farmer and rural area has almost been blank. There was even lack of financial support for the basic rice planting. It was estimated by Enping Agricultural Bureau that in 2006, the budget for spring ploughing would be about 50.4 million yuan, but farmers had only 11.8 million at hand, so there would still be a financing deficit up to 38.6 million.

Incomprehensive Agricultural Insurance: Farmers Taking on All Financial Risks

"Enping is located in the Pearl River Delta, so there is a broad market for planting and farming industries with the convenient transportation," said by Feng Langqi, deputy director general of Enping Agricultural Bureau. He believed that planting and farming required not only technologies and fundings but also agricultural insurance.

But agricultural insurance is incomplete and incomprehensive. It is known that since 2006, Enping insurance industry has seldom invested in the agricultural projects with low benefits and now, due to long time loss, it has stopped some tentative agriculture insurance. The lack of agriculture insurance to effectively withstand risks and unestablished correspondent risk compensation system further restrict financial institution's investment in agricultural construction and this has fallen into a vicious circle.

In 2006, Professor Yunus, known as "the poor's banker", won Nobel Peace Prize for his establishment of rural banks. The news inspired Chinese people and a new reform policy for opening rural financial market was brewing.

In December 2016, China Banking Regulatory Commission introduced a new policy which for the first time allowed industrial and private capitals to establish banks in rural areas and advocated setting up three financial institutions: village banks, finance corporations and rural mutual cooperatives. This attempt was considered as the ice−breaking move in the fourth−round of China's rural finance reformation.

Zhang Yuanhong, researcher of the Rural Development Institute of Chinese Social Academy College, said that: "Petty loan is very difficult to apply and this is a ubiquitous phenomenon in China rural areas." He also suggested with profits being the main targets of banks and a more intensive cost settlement, dispersed rural outlets were contracted and the examination and approval authority was centralized. Now, banking outlets under county−levels basically don't have the power to examine and approve loans.

Let Finance Return to Rural Areas

In fact, the lack of financial service in villages has already drawn attention from in society.

In 2009, there were over 60 villages with non−banking financial institution networks, located mainly in eastern, western and northern Guangdong and regions with underdeveloped economy or small−scale financial industries. Between 2010 and 2013, Guangdong had gradually filled the gap of non−banking financial institution networks in these villages by impelling new pilot types and scopes of rural finance institutions and encouraging commercial banks and rural credit cooperatives to set up new outlets.

The model of village banks were also introduced to China and piloted within a small range. By the end of 2007, Guangdong had officially started to make plans for the pilot work of new rural financial institutions and Enping and Ruyuan were selected as the first pilot regions. In March 2009, HSBC Enping Village Bank had a grand opening and it introduced a "corporation plus farmers" petty loan service. It provided loans for farmers and distributors who had frequent business transactions with the local leading enterprises, focusing on meeting the financial demands of Enping's rural and urban residents and rural micro and middle and small–sized enterprises.

In order to bring development to agriculture, farmer and rural area, China is currently proposing a series of policies: encouraging commercial bank share system to extend to countryside, initiatively providing farmers with petty loans and helping develop production. In the well–prepared and highly–developed regions, banking outlets are set up to facilitate farmers with loan transactions. Implementing new rural financial system

On 14 June, 2012, municipal leaders of Peijiang District, Jiangmen are spearheading an effort to donate for Poverty Alleviation Campaign. Members from all social sectors in Jiangmen actively participate in the campaign. On the day before, a written proposal was released to encourage people to join in the activity. Photo taken by Chen Zhuoda.

and establishing rural household organizations and petty loan corporations are measures to facilitate farmers' loan—applying.

Some poor regions lack in effective mode of economic development, thus financial capitals are hard to be invested and sustainability is not formed. Facing the chronic problems that hinder poor areas from overcoming poverty, such as difficulties in mortgage guarantee, insufficient guarantee pawn and unqualified borrowers, Guangdong banking industry has innovatively launched financial products suitable for rural comprehensive reformation and given a helped ease farmers' difficulties in borrowing money from banks.

In order to clear up the difficulties in guarantee, Guangdong Qingyuan Bank has launched a new "flow loan" targeting at 800 households with contractual rights of land. Li Liang, vice president of the Qingyuan Outlet of Agricultural Bank of China, suggested that: "On the basis of issuing certificates for contractual rights of land, farmers can apply for loans from village banks as needed and transform land resources to loan capitals."

After learning about local conditions, Guandong Yingde Rural Credit Cooperative released a loan product "adapted for farmers" , which moderately relaxed the restriction that borrowers must register in industry and commerce department. A credit line of two million yuan was allocated to farmlands from the rural credit cooperative in Yewu village, Shigutang Town, Yingde, to support land circulation and enhance land utilization rate.

To realize targeted poverty alleviation, Guangdong Provincial Party Committee starts a mode of "staying in village for poverty relief plus establishing cards for archives" and actively promotes "planning for every household and responsibility on every individual" in the province. A fixed three—year period is set for residential poverty alleviation groups to help villagers get rid of poverty.

This mode provides specialized petty loans for archived poor households to ensure funds are used for production and employment. Guangdong Banking Regulatory Commission encourages banking financial institutions to provide loans of no more than 50,000 yuan and within three years for archived poor households who have the willingness to borrow, the potential to start a business and professional skills on the basis of accurately evaluating these households' credit ratings and repayment abilities. The loans can be used to satisfy their demands for production, start-ups, employment and relocation and are with preferential interest rates.

Technology Accelerates Poverty Alleviation

Poor Household Selling Cherry Tomatoes on Taobao

On the Spring Festival of 2006, Super Cold Wave stroke southern China, and most regions in Guangdong was attacked by snow, resulting in the reduced production of weather−dependent farm produce. However, in places such as Zhanjiang, Qingyuan, instead of getting drastically shrinking earnings, some farmers from poor villages even obtained better incomes than ever. It is the "E−commerce Poverty Alleviation" and "Mobile Internet Poverty Alleviation" advocated and spread out by cadres of poverty relief campaign that have brought this change to villagers.

Tangtou villager Luo Ruting has received several boxes of orders for cherry tomatoes just after the Spring Festival and was preparing to harvest fruit in the fields for delivery. Due to the cold weather some seedlings were dry and shrunken. "We didn't have much fruit this year. If we pick some up this morning, then it can be delivered to Guangzhou in the afternoon." Luo casually picked up some bunches of light−red cherry tomatoes and told us: "Fruits sold on market are picked up before they are fully mature because they will naturally become ripe on the way of transportation so that buyer can have the best taste."

The breed of cherry tomato Luo Ruting plants is called "Millennium". It was introduced to Tangtou village from Hainan in 2014 by the poverty relief team in Zhanjiang when they found the information on E−commerce platform. By the introduction of "Millennium", the embarrassing situation of Tangtou's cherry tomatoes began to change.

By 2013, Luo could barely earn enough money to pay for his wife's medical expenses and children's tuition fees from the tens of thousands of units of "Wanfu" cherry tomatoes he planted because wholesalers always cut down the purchasing prices. Luo Zhu, committee member of village party branch said: "In the past, cherry fruit could only be sold at fifty cents per jin, but now the purchasing price for Millennium is at least one yuan, one can earn 15,000 yuan for every unit of fruit."

Luo Ruting, who used to be unfamiliar with smart phones, is now proficient in operating E−commerce processes and is responsible for taking orders and organizing delivery. He showed us the page of an online shop called "Zhanjiang Residential Poverty Alleviation Group Franchised Store", which has a wide variety of agricultural produce.

"The signals in the fields aren't so good so we usually check orders on the computer of the village committee," said Luo. He also told us since there is only one computer in the committee, it is planning to buy some new computers with the municipal grants.

He said, with a sense of proud: "Our cherry fruit is the best seller on the market and we have orders from Beijing, Tianjin and Shanghai." Now, the sources of Tangtou's cherry fruit orders have covered the Pearl River Delta. Once receiving an order, Luo will organize purchase and send the products by delivery or shuttle bus. He took scores of orders and went to Guangzhou for four times to deliver goods in December 2015 alone.

Cen Yukang is a cadre of Tangtou's poverty alleviation group and the initiator of "farm produce E-commerce". In the eyes of the villagers, he is a capable young man with medium height, a pair of glasses and a gentle look. Cen thinks the land conditions in Tangtou are very bad since most of them are unfertile sands and the village has an underdeveloped agricultural irrigation system. To Cen, with 105 poor households out of the 303 households in the village, the load of poverty alleviation task is very heavy.

"After arriving at the village the biggest problem we found was that farmers couldn't learn about the news on the market and they used the old planting technologies to plant agricultural products, including cherry fruit," said Cen. "In the past the seedlings of cherry fruit were all provided by buyers, and besides forcing down prices, they would also deduct a fee of 10% of rotten fruit. Even though some farmers could make a profit, that was not enough for them to get rid of poverty."

Cen was reminded of the vigorous developing trend of mobile Internet in big cities. And on 25 March, 2014, "Tangtou Poverty Alleviation Farm Produce Franchised Store" was officially launched on Taobao and Tangtou thus became the first village that made attempts to relieve poverty by using E-commerce.

According to the notice of China's Ministry of Industry and Information, the domestic users of mobile phone and mobile Internet will reach 1.28 billion and 980 million respectively in 2016. Mobile Internet has exerted a profound influence upon people's lives.

Taobao is a highly popular online retail platform in China owned by Alibaba Group, a company listed in America. At present, the website has nearly 500 million registered users, over 60 million fixed visitors every day, more than 800 million items in the online shops and averagely sells 48,000 products per minute. And the daily active users on Wechat have reached 670 million. Now people in big and mid-size cities needn't bring cash and

E-commerce changes the sales model of farm produce. Farmers use E-commerce to expand market and realize poverty alleviation.

credit cards when they go out since consuming places such as restaurants, clothes shops and supermarkets are connected with Internet payment, and consumers can use mobile phones to complete payment even in hospitals, taxis, parking lots and highways.

Cen told us: "At first, the farmers and poor households in the village don't know about E−commerce and they think it is too virtual to actually help them do business." In order to let villagers trust "E−commerce" ,

Cen met up with the biggest local purchaser and cooperated with him by selling cherry tomatoes for poor households on Taobao. It turned out that they helped sell 30,000 jins of "Wanfu" cherry tomatoes in the first half of 2014 alone. At the same time, Cen and the other members learned from the Internet about the "Millennium" cherry tomato in Hainan, which had a higher value as few places in China planted it. So the residential cadres bought grafted seedlings from Hainan, constructed a 100-unit of "Millennium" base and invited experts from Hainan to give technological training to poor households working in the base. After the New Year's Day of 2015, a large amount of "Millennium" cherry fruit was on the market and sold in Taobao shops, attracting plenty of buyers. In the same year, the base earned an income of over 200 million yuan, with 700,000 yuan paying to poverty-stricken farmers as salaries for picking and packaging. In January 2016, the purchasing price for the cherry tomato was up to 7.5 yuan per jin. Since October 2015, almost every villager had begun to plant "Millennium" and the planting area had increased from 100 to 350 units of fields.

As early as October 2014, the farm produce experience of Tangtou village was promoted to all the 95 poverty-stricken villages in Zhanjiang by the residential poverty alleviation team and the name of the Taobao shop was converted into "Zhanjiang Residential Poverty Alleviation Franchised Store" . In the shop, all the farm products from the 95 villages are shown. Things like cherry fruit, muskmelon, black rice, red rice, black goat, pitaya and seafood can all be found.

Now, all the farmers on Leizhou Peninsula are starting to plant "Milennium" cherry fruit and the planting areas have reached over 3,000 units of fields. Through E-commerce Poverty Alleviation, the cadres and villagers have built bases for green date, muskmelon and pitaya, with the areas of over 6,000 units. Besides, they have also brought in some good quality farm produce such as black rice, red rice and East No.1 honeydew melon and produced well−received sesame and peanut oil.

By the end of February 2016, by connecting with the markets in the Pearl River Delta, Yangzte River Delta and Beijing−Tianjin−Hebei Region, the online and offline sales volume of the agricultural produce in Zhanjiang areas had outnumbered tens of millions yuan. The residential poverty alleviation team in Zhanjiang also established a mode of "E−commerce platform + Storage and processing industrial base + cooperatives + farmers" . This mode had provided a good platform for local poor villages to establish a steady and effective poverty relief system in the long run. It was estimated that 30,000 poverty−stricken households in the Zhanjiang regions had benefited from E−commerce Poverty Alleviation.

Now Tangtou villagers like Luo Ruting and Luo Zhu have been familiar with the processes of selling agricultural products online and the three−year "E−commerce Poverty Alleviation" has brought a huge "E−commerce effect" in the 95 poor villages in Zhanjiang. Residential cadres also help villagers establish a farmers' specialized cooperative comprised of 12 households, which have been leading the development for another 88 households.

From May to August in 2015, Cen Yukang was invited by Shenzhen Training Base of the State Council National Cadres in Poverty−stricken Areas to teach E−commerce poverty alleviation to cadres in seven provinces and districts— Xizang, Yunnan, Jiangxi, Henan, Hunan, Hubei and Guangdong. In the eyes of Cen, E−commerce poverty alleviation was just an exploration to "Internet + Agriculture" mode. Only by the propulsion from the national level could the technological revolution of farm produce in poverty−stricken areas be truly carried out.

He believed the officials should establish an agricultural database as soon as possible, which should be open to agricultural enterprises and common farmers. He said: "For big E-commerce platforms, statistics such as climates, farm produce prices, comparisons among regional products and seedlings sold by sellers should be accessible to farmers. If not, then the government can buy these data from the platforms and make them open to farmers."

"Village Head's Rice" on Suning.com

Located in Chonglou town, Taishan, Qianfeng is a poverty—stricken village where residents make their living on farming. How to better sell the rice villagers plant has been a "long—existing difficult" problem. Due to the flowing back of the sea water and large portion of salt land, the collective income of the village has been stagnant. Three years ago, Jiangmen residential poverty alleviation group arrived here and has been working out different ways to help villagers eliminate the difficulties in selling farm produce.

The team leader of Chongfeng's poverty alleviation group Tan Junyan found that most villagers failed to take the initiative. As a result, the group invited a new village lead Liao Jieliang, a young man of the generation after 80s. Leaving his hometown as a migrant worker at a young age, Liao has always dreamed of applying his experience accumulated in the outer world to construct his village. Liao learned that the 1,800 people in Qianfeng village had a total of 1,700 units of fields and that was an average of less than one unit per person. Besides these, there were also 1300 units of banana patches and 280 units of forest. Apart from the elderly and kids, 60% of the young people were migrant workers. Liao said: "Farm produce is the major source of income for poor households and by finding markets for these products, the problems of low incomes could be solved."

Served by the government as a bridge, the operation team of Suning. com's Chinese Specialty Pavilion Taishan Branch arrived at Qianfeng and purchased all the village's rice patches, which relieved villagers' worries about the future. He Hengqing, head of operations in the Taishan Branch said: "The problems of unsalable potatoes in Jiangmen in 2015 inspired us to launch the farm produce campaign with Suning.com and we sincerely hope that, combining with Taishan's poverty alleviation purposes and goals, we can change the embarrassing situations of agricultural products in poverty—stricken villages."

Taishan also launched an online "Poverty Alleviation APP" . The APP gathers most of the information about poor villages and households and carries out various targeted poverty alleviation activities. It breaks the traditional mode of assistance and a series of O2O low—cost mutual—assistance campaigns will be launched in this channel.

It is known that recently the first assistance activity on this APP was "The Love Basket" , which was put on the "Public Crowd funding" column. The high quality farm produce from 920 poor households were picked up and packaged as " Love 99 Happiness Basket" (the number 9 means permanence in China). There were altogether 1,000 baskets and 99 yuan for each. All the earnings were given back to poor households to ease their selling plight.

The "Path" for
Online Job Hunting at Hand

"Just use a pen and fill in the application form, then you can wait for job opportunities coming to you at home. This will spare you a lot of trouble." Recently, Lian Chengjian, a poor villager in Wanzhong, Hekou town just received a copy of this "Job Application Form". In fact, in order to promote targeted poverty alleviation, Xinxing county has introduced a real time human resource recruitment platform—Taoli Network Techonology Co., Ltd (abbreviated as "Taoli" below), which made the "online job application form" tailored to situations of poverty−stricken households.

Under the instructions of residential cadres, Lian Chengjian completed some resume questions such as personal information, work experience and employment intention. Lian told us that the cadres would upload his resume to Taoli platform to conduct job matching and that he could receive job information through mobile phones sent by the platform. He said: "Once successfully matched, I could accept an offer of employment."

Graduated from junior college, Lian Chengjian is a 22-year-old man worn out by "difficulties in job hunting". Compared with aimlessly submitting CVs on all kinds of recruitment websites, by having residential cadres input personal information and conducting real time job application through Taoli platform, villagers meet with less unnecessary problems and get more chances to be employed.

Lian Chengjian illustrated this point by citing an example: After his graduation, he sent over 100 copies of his resume on all job hunting websites and mobile software but were rebuffed again and again due to insufficient education background and lack of experience. And now he works in a Guangzhou-based company and with an intern salary of 2,300 yuan every month, he could have nothing left excluding daily expenses.

Lian says he hopes to find a better job through Taoli platform and his expected wage welfare is over 3,000 yuan. He told us: "If my monthly wage is more than 3,000 yuan, then I can send more money back home to get rid of the poor conditions as soon as possible."

According to overall inspection, by the end of June, there are 7,054 poverty-stricken households (16,681 people) in Xinxing county and to realize comprehensive poverty alleviation, the major issue is to solve the employment of 2446 households (9,569 people) with work labor and let them get rid of poverty by employment.

However, due to the restricting factors of geographical locations, transportation and backward information, poor households rely mainly on relatives' and friends' recommendations and it is fruitless for them to look for jobs in cities. Helping poverty-stricken households' employment has become the key point and difficulty of the three-year targeted poverty alleviation campaign. Xinxing introduces Taoli Network Technology Co., Ltd to help solve the employment issues of poor households. The Taoli platform adopts an "Internet + Labor employment" mode and operates in an O2O pattern facing all the archived household labor and send information of job positions to them through mobile phones. At the same time, poor households can also enhance their techniques by attending Taoli's vocational trainings so as to find better jobs and earn higher salaries. The staff in Xinxing Poverty Alleviation Office Zhang Zhijun told us that in order to create more job opportunities, Xinxing and Taoli has signed a strategic cooperation contract with Taoli employment platform and the latter has set up Xinxing's targeted poverty relief project group. The two parties have conducted several researches on how to provide job descriptions and professional training for poverty-stricken households.

Considering that some poor villagers don't have smart phones, Taoli prepares and prints paper job application forms for them. In this way, households can either have residential cadres post their resumes on Taoli real time recruitment platform by submitting paper forms or conduct the process by themselves on the phones.

At present, Xinxing county is holding a "Labor Force Employment Poverty Alleviation Project" training and work advancement meeting, inviting the residential cadres and major secretaries from 15 major villages. By the end of this year, Taoli will provide several job positions for poor households, such as housekeeping job for women between 18 and 50, and positions for technicians, general workers, warehouse keepers, QA inspectors, welders and electricians.

High-speed Railways Have Changed the Lifestyles in Mountain Areas

High-speed Railways
Bring Popularity and Wealth

In the early summer, it is breezy and sunny in Guizhou. The tea growers are busy working in the green tea gardens as in previous years. And at the other end of the Guizhou−Guangdong high−speed railways, people are working speedily in front of computers to find market for the tea. This is a new change. With the development of technological information and transportation facilities, the tea growers in Guizhou and wholesalers in Guangdong are taking the "cloud" of Internet big data to enhance the credibility of Guizhou tea's quality safety and use the Internet to do big businesses. At the same time, with the opening of Guizhou−Guangdong high−speed railway and the integration into the three−hour economic circle in the Pearl River Delta, the trend of tea industry relieving poverty is rising.

Railway is the "artery" of the national economy. For years, besides ensuring people's convenient travelling, the railways have also played an important role in boosting economic development in poverty−stricken areas. In China, there is a sentence going like "Once the railway is opened, piles of gold could be got" . It shows railways' crucial role in connecting lines of the economic "arteries" around the nation.

Back in 1998, when the Guangzhou—Meizhou—Shantou railway was first opened, the counties along the road—Longchuan, Wuhua, Xingning and Fengshun were all "state—level poverty—stricken counties" , but by 2016, all these counties had got rid of the old label. With the advancement of speed and performance of the Guangzhou—Meizhou —Shantou railroad and the gradual construction of Hui—Mei—Shan high—speed railway, the counties along the high—speed railway lines would face another good chance for development.

Simultaneously, there has been a "big industrial zone" in the areas along the Wuhan—Guangzhou railway opened in 2009. By now, the

The opening of Wu-Guang high-speed railway.

railway has been in operation for six years and the cities alongside the railway lines such as Shaoguan, Qingyuan and the ones along the Xiang– Er high–speed railway have undertaken over 10,000 projects transferred from the Pearl River Delta, with a total investment of over 500 billion yuan. In 2015, the GDP growth rates of cities like Qingyuan and Shaoguan, which are located along the high–speed railway, were all above 8% and the amount of increase was higher than those of any other cities in the province.

The "Zoo" on the Trains

In the past, the train connecting Guizhou and Guangdong took more than 18 hours to travel through 857 kilometers. The "slow trains" between Guizhou and Guangdong have been operating for almost half a century since the 19th century. Liu Wencheng, who often travelled by this train in the past remembered that many passengers would sit around in the last carriage of the train—the baggage car, with several pack baskets of live chickens piling up beside them. For the 61-year-old Liu Wencheng, he couldn't have been more familiar with this train line.

It was twenty years ago that he took this train to Guangdong to sell the tea leaves collected from the mountains in Guizhou. And twenty years later, he is still relying on this train to gain wealth. Every half a month, Liu and some of his friends will carry the tea leaves and walk for over an hour to catch the train heading for Guangdong by 13:01. The wholesale price for the tea is 20 yuan/jin and retail price 30. Deducting the fare, Liu can earn 500 yuan for one trip.

The several thousand yuan Liu earned from selling tea has become an important complement of his family incomes. With a sense of satisfaction about the convenience the railway has brought to her, Liu told us: "We can only earn money when there is convenient transportation and low ticket prices."

Twenty years ago, besides tea leaves, there were crowds of yelling ducks and geese and battling goats in the end of the carriages, which formed a scene of "zoo" . While people were talking with each other, a goose might lay an egg and caused wild laughters on the train.

Actually at that time, in order to facilitate Guizhou's minority villagers' traveling to trade fairs with cattle, some trains in Guangdong made specific "baggage carriage" to place cattle and large luggage and there were ladders for cattle to get on and off the trains. The "slow trains" for poverty alleviation here used to be an important "engine" to impel economic development in the regions along the road and improve people's living standards.

But now the "slow trains" have disappeared and the mission of the "baggage carriage" have ended. A high–speed railroad with an hourly speed of 350 kilometers is connecting Guizhou with Guangdong and the travelling time between the two provinces has shortened from 21 hours to 5 and a half.

In Hetaoba, Meitan county, Guizhou, 40 years of tea planting has relieved villagers from poverty and their life has changed from "living on brown rice and traveling over mountains for water" into "water is at hand and electricity–powered" . With the opening of Guizhou–Guangdong high–speed railway, villagers have built dams, tea gardens and roads and later established brands, associations and Internet sales. Just within a few years, the tea farmers, who used to live on weather, have targeted their visions at broader markets.

Jing Linbo is a Hetaoba villager who has been engaged in tea business for more than ten years. Besides owning a tea company, he also constructed a 6-unit tea-making workshop and is in charge of growing tea, purchasing and processing tea leaves.

However, the young man isn't satisfied with only doing a tea retailing and wholesaling business. Excluding costs, he can only earn a profit of 10 or 20 yuan per jin and the prospects for increasing profits are slim since prices are continually forced down by buyers. Jing Linbo believes that he needs to move from the bottom of the market and is determined to build his own brand. Ever since the Guizhou-Guangdong high-speed railway was opened, the costs for transportation has dramatically went down and as more people and products circulate in the area, tea farmers finally get rid of the trouble brought about by inconvenient traffic and Hetaoba village is beginning to step out of poverty.

Meitan county is a major tea-production area in Guizhou, and with a planting area of more than 500,000 units, the overall income of tea industry in 2014 reached over 3 billion yuan. As the origin of Meitan's tea industry and tea culture, Hetaoba village particularly "thrives on tea industry". There are 10,000 units of tea gardens in the village, and 868 households are planting or processing tea. And the well-known Hetaoba tea leaves are purchased by tea dealers in large amount.

In 2014, the average income of local farmers reached 14,200 yuan per person, but more and more tea farmers are no longer satisfied to be the ring with lowest profits in the industrial chain. The Internet thus becomes a "powerful weapon" for tea growers to develop new markets. Since the end of 2014, Liu Shengyan, a tea grower, has been busy opening subscription accounts and service accounts to deliver news about "Yunxiang Tea" and let more people know about Xiangmei green tea by transmitting through beautiful words and pictures. Currently, dozens of corporations in Hetaoba have established their own online distribution channel on big E−commerce platforms such as TMALL and JD. COM and are making higher sales volume year by year.

How to convert tea−planting into an industry and change his own role from tea grower to tea dealer are questions Liu Zeyuan wants to answer. He is planning to unite with the leading tea−processing companies in the village to set up a tea "gathering company" . It aims at realizing no cutting−down of prices and no purchasing on credit in order to solve the problems of insufficient investment capitals and slow withdrawal of funds. At present, every year the county will have many tea growers and production enterprises take part in all kinds of domestic farm produce trade fair and tea exposition to let them find business opportunities.

Targeted Poverty Alleviation of High-speed Railways Free for Special Passengers

On 18 January, 2017, before Chinese Lunar New Year, four "Trains of Happiness" , leaving successively from Guangzhou and Shenzhen, took over 3,000 migrant workers back home to Guangxi, Guiyang, Hubei and Hunan.

Jishou in Hunan, Baise in Guangxi and Guiyang in Guizhou are all the poverty alleviation assistance areas of Guangdong. The K9064 train from Shenzhen to Jishou is a specialized line for the poverty alleviation campaign. Before passenger transport during the Spring Festival, Guangzhou Railway Group, with the help of the news media, sent out messages that Guangdong Human Resources and Social Security Office and benevolent enterprises would donate free train tickets for migrant workers from Jishou, Shibadong and the neighboring villages. The Group arranged railway conductors of Jishou origin to perform crew services and hold charity activities on the trains.

Liang Yongning, who took on crew services work, was a disable man, the initiator of the charitable organization "Come

Back Home Baby" and was rated as one of the ten most influential public figures in charity by Sina Weibo in 2016. He personally donated 10 train tickets to help the migrant workers from Shibadong go back home and celebrate the Spring Festival. One among those who received a free ticket was a retired soldier called Duan Guangming. He is working in a electronics factory in Shenzhen and with a monthly salary of 5,000 yuan, his family's living standard is gradually improving.

The "motorcycle army" that needs to be taken care of every year. can also benefit from the convenience provided by the high-speed railways. As the restrictions of motors in Guangdong, Guangxi and Guizhou have become increasingly common, the high-speed rail accommodation power has increased by 20% in 2016 and could transfer 70,000 passengers every day. Therefore, on the basis of continuing to open specialized lines for motorcycle army, the benevolent high-speed railway opened in 2016 can bring more safety and convenience to the way home of "motorcycle army".

Characteristic Towns: It's Nice Living in Mountain Villages

Transition of the "Great Northern Wilderness" in Guangzhou

Lianma village, Lvtian, which is located in the northernmost of Guangzhou, borders on Xinfeng, Shaoguan in the north and Longmen, Huizhou in the east and is called as the "north door" of Guangzhou. In recent years, the fresh air and beautiful natural sceneries in Lianma has attracted attention to its tourism resources. And as Lianma being listed into Conghua district's "beautiful town" construction project, the village has taken on a new look and got rid of the old image of a poverty—stricken area. With the changes brought forth by the project, the lives in the mountains have become better and better. In the near future, living in mountains could become something the city dwellers dream about.

Lianma is Guangzhou's largest administrative village with 11 economic unions and a population of 1,406. The lands in Lianma are mainly in mountainous regions and due to the restrictions of geographical features, farmers can only grow produce such as "Sanhua Plum" and "sugar oranges" rather than regular vegetables.

The design of Lianma's ecological rainwater garden.

Pan Guangzao, party branch secretary of Lianma told us: "In the past, villagers made most of living on forest resources, but later the government issued strict policies to protect forests so the traditional mode of forest−oriented income system was broken. Villagers could only earn a slim income by charging for protecting the water resources in protected forests, and much of capable work labor chose to work outside." As the village was remote and with a low living standard, it was regarded as the "Great Northern Wilderness" by locals in Conghua.

The embarassing situations in Lianma brought much concern to town and village cadres. How to effectively integrate and utilize current resources and find out a development model suitable for the village were the questions they want to answer. In the end of 2014, the leaders of Guangzhou made a survey about Lianma and pointed out its directions for developing ecological tourism, which brought new opportunities to the village. In 2015, Conghua district made the decision of converting Lianma into a "beautiful town" and this brought a "wind of change" to the village and gave out abundant fruit in a year's time. Since July 2013, Guangzhou has started three−year assistance to Lianma village, which brought a new appearance to it. In 2016, the collective income of Lianma has reached 565,300 yuan, with the 20 poor households earning an average annual income of 15,000 yuan, the place has turned into wealthy village .

The construction of "beautiful town" has brought breathtaking changes to Lianma and villagers suggest that the most evident ones are improved environment and increased incomes.

Since construction of infrastructure is the biggest livelihood project, the construction and improvement of Liansheng village exactly started with building facilities that benefit people. Pan Guangzao introduced to us that in the past year, Lianma gradually formed the construction scale of beautiful villages and there were great changes in the building of basic infrastructure, which included the expanding construction of roads, riverbanks, lanes, parking lots and sewage facilities. At present, a four−mile riverbank and 12−mile lane construction have already been completed and the 3.1−mile long social road linking G105 and Huangshakeng Economic Union has been asphalt−paved. In terms of environment, there are a lot of newly−added landscapes near the village committee, which brings the place a refreshing look.

From Farmers to B&B Shopkeepers

Now a one-hour drive on the highway takes tourists directly from Guangzhou to Lianma and the gradual openings of highways have brought this northern mountainous village a lot of popularity and business opportunities. In September 2016, the college student's art hotel invested by Guangzhou Huaxia Vocational College announced its formal commencement for construction. The project was planned to last for three months, and with a total investment of 6 million yuan, it aimed at promoting local economic development by vitalizing spare farm houses to build modernized and ecological art bases.

Not far from the art hotel, some B&B accommodations are being built. The hotel called "Lanwu" standing right beside the village committee building is quite eye-catching. Walking into it, you can feel a natural sense of village life and the decorations are beautiful yet full of rural characteristics. This is the first B&B in Lianma, which was converted from the villager Chen Huichun's house.

Since the trial operation in the end of 2015, Chen's B&B has enjoyed great welcome from tourists. In the past, Chen was only an ordinary housewife and was responsible of planting vegetables and doing chores at home. But now, with the rapid development of "Lianma Town" , she has become a "shopkeeper" and earned a steady income.

The relative responsible officials in Lvtian town suggest that local government will choose 10 farm houses to build family stay as pilots and they will be operated in a "government + village collectivity + farm households" mode with a moderate support from fiscal capitals. These family stays will be uniformly managed by Guangzhou Beijingyuan Tourism Development Co., Ltd, which is a company established by the village and by doing so, irregular development and malicious competition between Lianma home stays can be avoided.

Besides B&Bs, the construction of peanut oil workshops and hotels designed by Guangzhou Art College painters which feature in urban agriculture and culture tourism is also under the way. Among these, Lianma Conference Center and Youth Hostel, which can accommodate 300 tourists, will be completed in 2017. At present, Chen Huichun is negotiating with other villagers to enlarge the management scope of farm stays and seize the business opportunities during the National Holiday. She is hopeful about the village's development: "In the future, more distinctive cultural and tourism facilities will be built in Lianma."

The northward ancient post road in Lianma is only left 300 meters long and the village committee has rebuilt it according to the few descriptions in the historical books. The village secretary Pan Guangzao hopes that the renovated road can "tell" the ancient stories in Lianma. The officials in Lvtian said: "Introducing projects doesn't mean earth–shaking removal and construction, it means sticking to the traditions and preserving the ecological distinctiveness of the town." Actually, right at the beginning of the construction, the village invited a team of China Rural Construction Institute to work out the plans of establishing a beautiful town, which focused on keeping rural characteristics.

Pan Guangzao told us: "Lianma tofu and peanut oil, as local special farm products, enjoy a high popularity and introducing corporations to upgrade farmers' production in industrial measures can not only enlarge production scale, but also demonstrate the traditional production arts." He also revealed that now the white spirit workshop had already invited masters in Wuliangye to teach the way of making liquor and refining the cultural values of brewage.

Conghua businessman Luo Ting has been looking for new investment opportunities for years and he came back to his hometown Lianma on the Spring Festival after leaving the place for more than a decade. With a sharp sense of business opportunities, he decided to return to his hometown and invest in urban agriculture. He said: "The construction in the town is in full swing and one can find opportunities everywhere." His first step is to renovate farm houses and invite designers to plan for farm stays and the second one is to develop green gardens by cooperating with villagers to plant and breed and develop urban agriculture with local characteristics. From traditional iron and steel trade to modern agriculture, Luo Ting has found a sticking point in Lianma to make the transformation from traditional capital to new business type. And by utilizing the advantaged ecological environment in Guangzhou, more and more investors like Luo Ting have drawn their capitals to the high—quality ecological resources of Lianma. Currently, many corporations have settled in Lianma and the green farm produce from the origins of Liuxi River and the farmhouse cultural products will enter the Pearl River Delta.

Start-ups
Accelerate "Town" Construction

As the National Holiday approaches, Pan Anna, a post—80s girl, has to step up the purchase of goods in the neighboring areas in order to welcome the peak flow. After graduating from college in 2006, Pan used to work in the town government. In the end of 2015, she chose to settle in Lianma and established her first entrepreneurship project— "Beiyuan Home" .

"Bei means the northernmost of Guangzhou and Yuan means the origin of Liuxi River. We wish to make our customers feel at home." With a little investment, Pan Anna started with vitalizing adobe houses and renovated farm houses by decoration and repairment.

Since the end of 2015, "Beiyuan Home" has gained some popularity on the Internet and tourists have gained deeper impression of Lianma through its accommodation and services. Pan Anna told us as a small business start—up, she invested monthly profits to the hotel and infrastructure construction such as adding fences for streams and paving black bricks to gradually improve the neighboring environment.

Ecological tourism and modern agriculture add vitality to rural industries and the development opportunities brought by green economy have attracted many young people to come back to Lianma. Pan Guangzao said: "Learning that the development of specialized town is under way, more and more youngsters come to the village for opportunities and these include young villagers, students and some start−ups." He also told us that dozens of migrant workers had come back to the village and the change in demographic structure had added vitality to this mountainous village and the construction was accelerating.

Not all reforms could go smoothly. As for the changes in Lianma, villagers' incomprehension stems from unfamiliarity and their support stems from the feelings about the benefits brought by changes. Pan Guangzao said that the development orientation for Lianma was to build an ecological scenic spot. Therefore, constructing B&Bs, home−stays and village hotels will be one of the most important projects for Lianma from now on. With the influential power brought by advertisement, the quiet and clear natural environment in Lianma has attracted many tourists to come. Pan introduced to us: "At present, we have already opened three home−stays and once at weekends or on public holidays, swarms of tourists will come for specialized dishes and live here for some days. Since the Spring Festival, one shop has earned 100,000 yuan." In January 2016, the DaGuang highway was opened, which brought significant influence on Lianma. Under the efforts of committee cadres, the name of "Lianma" was added on the board of the exit of DaGuang highway, greatly adding the popularity of Lianma. Driving off from Lianma exit, one could arrive at the village with only a five−mile national road drive. Now it takes only 80 minutes to drive from Guangzhou central districts to Lianma, which is very fast and convenient. On the May Day Holiday in 2016, the home−

stays in Lianma was filled with tourists and the supply was unable to meet the demand.

In order to encourage villagers to support the development of construction and increase their initiatives for starting up their own business, the village committee also issued preferential policies to offer the top 10 households who took the lead in building B&Bs and home-stays a 50,000 yuan grant. At present, among all the projects in Lianma, when it relates to human resources and mechanical equipment, villagers will be firstly considered under the same conditions so as to increase their employment opportunities and incomes.

The Characteristic Town in Conghua Has Become the "New Engine" of Regional Innovation

On the last weekend of November 2016, the First Guangzhou Straw Festival was held in Xitang village. The theme of it was not only ecological tourism and leisure sightseeing but also the beginning of adding comic elements to the core districts of fairy tale town, which was the first cooperation of Animation Association and Xitang fairy tale town. Earlier these days the concerned department of the General Administration of Sports have officially signed a cooperation agreement of building a "national outdoor industry demonstration zone" with Conghua district. In the next five years, some big events and activities such as Guangzhou Camping Festival, Outdoor Activity Festival and National Mountaineering and Fitness Convention will be held in the characteristic town. Under the attraction of brand activities, streams of people, information and capitals from all over the country will connect with Conghua.

After the autumn harvest, Xitang village is covered with golden paddy fields. In the end of every November, the locals make the straws into simple scarecrows for entertainment. In

2016 the Straw Festival was upgraded into a urban—scale activity, which attracted enormous crowds of people and business opportunities.

Xitang is located in the northeast of Aotou town and is beside the S355 line. The village, which is approximately 4.2 square meters large, is 11 miles away from downtown Conghua in the east and 60 miles away from Guangzhou in the south and has a farm land of 1,998 units. In the past, the development in Xitang was extremely backward and most young man chose to work outside.

In the end of 2015, Xitang was listed into the Conghua's construction of characteristic town and defined as "fairy tale town". How to make this into reality? The related official in Aotou town told us: "The first step is to implement infrastructure construction and environment improvement, the second is to insert endogenous dynamics to development by introducing different corporations and lastly is to settle in comic elements and resources."

Chen Haitao, village secretary of Xitang told us: "Xitang is affluent in ecological resources and it is the locals' sincere hope to get through the channel from ecology to industries and bring vitality for rural development." In the beginning of 2016, Xitang gradually introduced three urbanized agriculture corporations and several months ago, some villagers began to return to the village for job opportunities and the once deserted village was alive again. Thirty local villagers became greenhouse workers and they need to take good care of vegetables and pack the vegetables into different family packages according to their requirements and eventually deliver these packages by cold chain to 200 households in Guangzhou.

"The actual aim of the Straw Festival is to earn popularity for the town and introduce more corporations to development a fairy tale tourism town centering on 'three rural issues' by melting with animation culture."

The related officials in Conghua revealed the "ambition" of the Straw Festival to us.

In 2016 the construction of 19 characteristic towns in Xitang has already entered the implementation stage. After the Straw Festival, Xitang will welcome a new round of reconstruction and will integrate resources to build some ecological science popularization bases such as "Seedling Kingdom" and "Insect Kingdom" to provide places for sketch and inspiration—stimuli for animation corporations.

Baoqu Rose World, Sakura Garden, Blossom Garden and several ecological tourism scenic spots decorate Xihe village with splendid seas of flowers and make it look like an amorous painting. With the impulsion of characteristic town project, the local government actively encouraged land circulation, which attracted several enterprises to settle in. The official in Xihe said that the local's agricultural production structure with high production and high added—value had realized the industrialization of flower production and enhanced the planting benefits. At present, 35 enterprises have settled in Xihe and as more than 10,000 units of land are already put into production, a flower production and sight—seeing industry featuring in producing fresh cut flowers, orchids, potted flowers, sakuras and characteristic seedlings have initially taken shape.

The official on Conghua suburban streets told us: "We plan to build Xihe into the most exotic town in Guangzhou and construct the only distinctive agricultural park in Guangdong here." From Lvtian in the north to the southern suburbs, several characteristic towns have preliminarily formed and taken on a different look.

By now, Conghua has built several characteristic towns according to the results of research. These include: the northernmost Lianma town featuring in camping and excursion, the southern amorous Xihe town built on flower resources, the Wenquan wealth town comprising characteristic finance, start—up innovation and romantic wedding and the Xitang fairy tale town targeting at children and parenting market.

Establishing Hundreds of Provincial Characteristic Towns in Guangdong by 2020

Characteristic towns mean the new development zones in the specified areas in cities and towns which integrate specialized industries and blend the functions of business, culture, tourism and living.

Focusing on distinctive leading industries and traditional industries, Guangdong will build nine characteristic towns. These towns will emphasize "character" and while keeping the industries distinctive, the patterns of the towns should also be distinctive.

In the meantime, the characteristic towns should also promote innovative entrepreneurship. In Zhejiang, where the promotion of distinctive towns is under way, the outcomes of effective investment and consumer enthusiasm have emerged. Taking Songshan Lake, Dongguan as an example, the local government is striving to build an "Internet+" town and actively improving the innovative start−up ecology by combining its industrial characteristics. And now the distinctive Internet industrial cluster has taken shape. The town aims at building a 2.2 million square meter start-up base and fostering 3-5 leading enterprises and 500 innovative small and medium-sized corporations in the Internet industry by 2018.

广东最穷村庄扶贫记：与石灰岩地貌的斗争

石灰岩山村的守望者

在电影《火星救援》里，在孤独的火星种着土豆的马特·蒙达面对的条件是极端艰苦。但至少他还有肥沃的火星土壤，为他孕育一季又一季的土豆。在孟山村，虽然不缺空气，可土壤、水等必需品却是稀罕物。

广东有石灰岩山区6208平方公里，占全省面积的3.5%，主要分布在粤北和粤西地区，粤东北有零星出现。这些地区有一个共同的特点，大部分都是广东最为贫困的地区。黎埠镇孟山村位于广东省北部的阳山县，属典型的石灰岩山区，山多地少，同时严重缺水，平均海拔500多米。7年前，驻村扶贫组进驻时的统计显示，全村378户中，有贫困户127户437人，低保五保69户171人。

孟山村为什么这么贫穷？我们先来看看孟山村的自然条件。作为山区，农民最重视的自然是土地。孟山村的田地全部分布在石灰岩土质的山坡上。石灰岩山区的典型地貌，带给这里的影响十分深刻。在孟山村，"石山"和"土山"的交错分布中，被切割得分散的小地块，几乎产不出经济效益。没有矿山，没有工厂，又无力改变自然，孟山村民在自然经济的脆弱中日复一日地艰难活着。

很多村民自己也难以用语言描述清楚自己家田地的位置和样子。当地最经典的自嘲式笑话是，有一天下雨，一农户披着斗笠上山耕地，到了地里，雨停了，农户将斗笠随手丢在了地上，然后一块块为自家土地翻土。可忙了一天，农户发现自家的土地少了一块。农户找了半天也没找到，临近傍晚，农户起身收行装准备回家。结果当他拿起斗笠的时候发现，斗笠下有一块小小地田，正是他刚刚漏掉的那块地。笑话有些夸张，可却反映出孟山村村民的尴尬。

其实这种尴尬在石灰岩地貌的山区十分常见。虽然地理面积大，但可利用的耕地面积却少得可怜。零星分布的耕地导致大面积种植以及工业化种植手段都无法应用在农作上。就算有一些能够耕种的土地，耕种的农作物也受到限制，高产值的农作物基本难以种植，只能种植木薯、玉米等农作物。

恶劣的环境还伴随着基础设施建设的极度匮乏。孟山村440亩水田中有285亩是"望天田"。用村委会主任陈金胜的话说，全年只能耕种一造，无法灌溉耕作。"眼看着天上下来雨水，却留不住。"

解决"望天田"，建设水利设施实现灌溉，村民们在扶贫帮扶组来之前，其实做梦都在想挖几口水塘，以解决农业灌溉和饮水问题。早在21世纪初，村民们曾经从深山挖了一条细沟，将石头缝里渗出的山泉水引到了山下。可由于财力有限，山泉水引下来后只流进了几口深约2米的蓄水池，等村民们用水管将蓄水池的水引到自家门口时，已经水量不多，渗不出几滴水了。

而要解决全村的饮用水问题必须挖塘打井，需要投资20万元，可让人尴尬不已的是，当时整个村子的村民经济收入主要靠外出打工及村民种植油茶零散作物，人均年收入仅为3000元，平时生活捉襟见肘，更不要说拿出多余的钱集资修建水利工程。

随着全球变暖，厄尔尼诺现象增强，世界银行曾作出警示会有1亿人因厄尔尼诺现象致贫。这1亿人就包括广东高海拔地区石灰岩山区的村民。

村民在石灰岩山区生活靠天吃饭，如果遇上雨雪旱涝等灾情，就更加毫无抵抗能力。村子里稍有能力的人，慢慢都选择搬迁了。在2013年前，孟山村一些村民小组，没有一栋新房，多数村民家都是建于上世纪30年代到50年代间的土坯房，土坯房外墙上还留着上世纪60年代的宣传标语。

"突围者"回不去的故乡

2016年中国的流动人口大军总数达到了2.45亿。流动人口是在中国户籍制度条件下的一个概念，指离开了户籍所在地到其他地方居住的人口，国际上，类似的群体被称为"国内移民"。中国流动人口的规模在改革开放后的30多年中持续增长，尤其是20世纪90年代以后增长速度明显加快，从1982年的657万人增长到2010年的2.2亿人，达到了前所未有的规模，占全国总人口的17%左右。北京、上海和广州等城市的当地常住居民中，约40%是流动人口。大部分流动人口是从农村流动到城市的年轻劳动力。

流动人口中有一部分人是看中大城市的机会，另一部分人则是因为家乡恶劣的生存环境而被迫背井离乡。如果人们在7年前来到清远市的一些大山贫困区会发现，沿着村路一路东行，村子里寂静无声，两边的房屋老旧残破，一些屋子呈现倾颓之势。村里大部分村民能走的都走了，留下来的都是老人和小孩，还有的是需要照顾老人没法出去打工的人。

这些山村在上一个十年中没有变化吗？其实几年前孟山村也有变化。在孟山村大部分村民眼中，近十年来，孟山村的变化仅限于：修通了一条砂石路和一栋两层的村委会办公楼。1997年，村民们凑了两万多块钱，终于打通了通往竹田、水塘等小组的砂石路。而建于1999年的村委会小楼，过了好几年，才找到孟山籍外出人员和扶贫单位赞助，还清建楼债务。

在先天贫瘠的地理条件和日渐频繁的天灾的双重挤压下，村里有能力者慢慢选择了迁移和流动来进行突围。可是突围并不顺利，外迁者大多无一技之长，想生存、发展、稳定也不容易，由于入户难，还遇到子女教育、就业、计划生育管理等一系列社会问题。

上世纪90年代，村里人第一次集体走出大山，去佛山顺德做拆楼工人。集体出走并没让村里人赚到财富，加之不习惯大山外面的生活，大部分壮劳力又回到了孟山村。67岁的熊火兰走了一条完全不同的道路。当时他没去做拆楼工人。他到邻近的连州捡垃圾谋生。熊火兰捡垃圾的工作和很多巴西贫民窟里垃圾回收工作一样。当时中国主要城市并未建立垃圾分类系统，这些拾荒者们把整个城市的垃圾捡回来，把垃圾里有用的可回收再利用材料分拣出来，进行二次变卖，让这些可回收再利用资源得到充分应用。踏实肯干，熊火兰在50多岁的时候讨到了老婆。在整个孟山村，像熊火兰这样在外打工赚到一点钱就搬迁的村民，在21世纪头十年慢慢多了。2000年12月份，孟山村全村人口1944人，到2009年底这一数字是1823人，除去少数死亡人口，人口减少基本是由于人口外迁。

可是外迁也不是一劳永逸，对这些外迁人口而言，面临的问题仍然存在，在由农村人向城市人的转变过程中，想要保证生存发展的持续稳定性并不容易。因为他们大多无一技之长。

扶贫就是让留守者坚定信心

石灰岩山区之穷是广东山区扶贫工作存在已久的困局。对类似孟山村这样的石灰岩山区而言，其本身生产资源极度匮乏，生存条件又极为恶劣，政府即便花费大力气在此采取一些开发型脱贫措施，其发挥的作用也十分有限。

从1997年开始，当地对石灰岩山区进行了一系列的帮扶工作，比如发放种植、养殖基金，帮助当地农户解决缺少资金投入生产等问题。但由于一些技术、销售困难的原因，最后"生产资金"大多成了"生活资金"，并未有效扭转当地的贫困态势。

如何盘活当地经济也是一门大学问。满山遍野的油茶树郁郁葱葱、洁白亮丽的茶花散发着淡淡的清香……这是孟山村现在的新面貌。自2009年初起，广东电网清远供电局、阳山县供销社出手，与黎埠镇孟山村结成帮扶伙伴，采取帮扶措施，在3年时间使该村127户贫困户基本实现脱贫。

当地村民细数了油茶前景，一亩可以种120株左右，每亩油茶年产油约200斤，即使按照20元/斤来算，一年就可以收入4000元。目前孟山村油茶种植面积大概有400亩左右，每户贫困户的种植规模分别在2~5亩不等。

油茶的挂果期需要3至5年，10年以后将进入盛果期，稳产收获期可达到80年以上。54岁的朱才英是家中唯一的劳动力，儿子成年却患上精神疾病；8年前老伴患癌症去世，10万多元的积蓄全部清空。"家里2亩多山地都转租给种植油茶的人，我收了租金还能为他们打工，随着油茶挂果越来越多，以后的收入会更高。"朱才英说。

金融手段助力最贫困山村

　　帮扶组带来了产业脱贫，也带来了金融扶贫。金融手段的创新也改变了广东贫困村的落后面貌。阳山县创造性地提出"扶贫经纪人"（自愿帮扶贫困户的村干部、能人大户）的概念。驻村干部物色为人勤奋老实、脱贫愿望强烈的贫困户，并让他们与能人大户结对。阳山扶贫办通过借款扶持"扶贫经纪人"扩大生产，再通过"扶贫经纪人"捆绑帮扶贫困户。

　　最重要的是，阳山县扶贫办为每个村庄在银行垫资10万元撬动50万元借款，由"扶贫经纪人"担保借款给贫困户。正是通过这样的金融创新，孟山村里竟然出现了好几个大型养殖基地。

　　村民面临着资金短缺的难题。为了帮孟山村筹集资金，帮扶单位创新性地设立了村级互助资金。

　　"村级互助资金就可以说是'村级银行'。"据阳山县扶贫开发办公室主任潘志伟介绍，村级互助资金主要由政府筹集，目前，政府已经为孟山村筹集了近40万元，贫困户无须存款，就可以借3000元。

"如果与龙头企业合作，还可以向农行申请不超过互助金5倍的借款。"潘志伟举例说，如一个贫困户最多可以借9000元，那么，他就可以向农行申请4.5万元的贷款。

当然，贫困户也并非可以随意到村级自助组织借款，需要大户担保，或者三户以上提供担保。"村级银行"打动了村民发展的心。村民江思文说，做一个猪舍、养300多头猪需要10万元。如果只靠自己，很难拿出那么多资金。而通过村级互助资金，自己终于可以贷款几万元，"我的目标是做达到千头猪规模的养猪场"。

弃贫：整体搬迁迎来新生

广东粤北山区是广东较早探索移民搬迁的地区。针对石灰岩地区特殊的地理环境和恶劣的生产生活条件，近十多年来，当地一直在通过有效的搬迁移民进行扶贫。当地比较成功的做法是，将搬迁人口迁移至划定的区域，并帮助搬迁人口寻找工作，解决子女上学问题。居民搬迁后，人均纯收入普遍提高，并基本融入安置地的生活。

韶关乳源瑶族自治县大桥镇中冲村地处深山，进出不易，一路上从高速转入国道，国道驶进乡间公路，公路变小路，最后才走进乡村。

这里是广东少数几个冬天下雪的地方，每年11月份之后，山上一片枯黄。虽说都是地处岭南，然而与温暖湿润的珠三角地区相比，这是一片沉睡的乡村。

如今这里的面貌和以前却大不相同，半山腰上的瑶族新村是中冲村村民整体搬迁出来建设的，从深山之中搬到县城的边沿，离县城只有3公里的距离，村口就是修建不久的环山公路，出入非常方便。

这次搬迁改变了村民的出行习惯，如果是2010年前，赵天香要想去一趟城里都是一件大事。他鸡鸣时分就得出发，走上4个小时的山路，到了县城，赶快置办完货品，就得马上回程。否则天黑以后，山路狭窄，悬崖陡峭，非常危险。

中冲村整体重建后，孩子可以进入县城的小学读书。新村是瑶族风格，每个村民的家有两层小楼，130平方米，白墙青瓦红栏杆，绘上瑶族的古老纹饰。离开深山，村民多了几条活路，现在可以务农，也可以务工。

2010年开始，中冲村开始种植高山蔬菜。现在全村有三个基地，即蔬菜、油茶和黄烟基地，其中高山蔬菜已经成为广东的一个品牌，种植的茄子、辣椒、豆角供应广州、深圳、东莞等地，中冲村所在的大桥镇已经成了珠三角的菜篮子。

中冲村只是广东贫困山区移民整体搬迁的一个缩影。早在上世纪90年代，广东就开始了庞大的移民整体搬迁工程。1994年—1997年，就有10万清远山区贫困村民实现了整体搬迁。2011年—2016年又有30万广东山区贫困农民异地搬迁。农民搬迁后，政府帮忙建设新房和配套措施，农民得以直接从自然条件恶劣的地区搬入经济较发达地区，享受当地的公共服务。

在最新出台的广东省扶贫政策中，有八大扶贫工程，其中之一就是要通过改善人居环境，巩固易地移民搬迁成果，支持安置区配套公共设施建设和迁出区生态修复；对不具备生产生活条件的零散分布的贫困户，实施插花搬迁；对没有搬迁意愿的少数贫困户，探索以生态补偿方式让其中有劳动能力的就地转化为护林员等生态保护人员。

教育扶贫：
扶贫先扶智

雷州的"撒哈拉沙漠"

中国大陆最南端的雷州半岛，西临北部湾，东涉南海，南隔18海里的琼州海峡与海南岛相望。5000—6000年前，雷州半岛这块红土地上，已有人类活动，秦时纳入华夏版图，古合浦郡治所在地。是汉王朝对外贸易重要基地，史称"海上丝绸之路"始发港。唐代后，李氏皇朝才有计划"徙闽民于合州"（唐贞观八年改合州为雷州）。宋以后南迁汉人（主要为闽南人居多）逐年递增，加速了雷州半岛之开发步伐。千百年生生息息的半岛人，创造了很多独特的非物质文化。雷州歌作为用雷州半岛的独特语言雷语方言演唱的歌曲是国家级非物质文化遗产。雷州半岛的独特语言与南粤大地，特别是经济富裕的珠三角地区的广府方言有很大区别。

位于粤西雷州半岛地区有一个东塘村，村里有一个走不出的怪圈，改革开放这么多年来，无论走出去多少打工的青壮年，都无法留在当地安心打工，到头来，全部都要回到这个全省闻名的贫困村里。

根据2010年统计，东塘村共有908户3957人，处于贫困线以下的有468户2021人，贫困率超过51%。按世界银行统计，30年前中国的整体贫困率约为53%。也就是说，这里的生活水平还停留在上世纪80年代。

在这片贫瘠的土地上，村支书王南干了整整13年。直到2010年，他才在两个弟弟的帮助下，告别茅草屋，盖上红砖房。

贫困，为什么会一直在这个小村庄停留衍生？扶贫又是怎么让贫困脱离这片土地？

撒哈拉沙漠是世界上除南极洲之外最大的荒漠，撒哈拉沙漠位于非洲北部，北到地中海，南到苏丹草原。位于阿特拉斯山脉和地中海（约北纬35°线）以南，约北纬14°线（250毫米等雨量线）以北。撒哈拉沙漠约形成于250万年前，是世界仅次于南极洲的第二大荒漠，也是世界最大的沙质荒漠，是地球上最不适合生物生存的地方之一。其总面积约容得下整个美国本土。而位于广东雷州半岛的东塘村常被人称为雷州的"撒哈拉沙漠"。

东塘村的自然禀赋可以用"恶劣"两个字来形容。土地贫瘠，严重沙化。雨季时，海风长驱直入，带来丰沛降水，田里的积水半年也排不完；但这里也会一连好几个月滴雨未下，村民只能眼睁睁看着禾苗干死。

进入21世纪，中国加大了对农业的投入力度，国家粮食收购价格节节攀升，广东稻谷每斤最低收购价逼近1元。但这一切，在2012年前和东塘人似乎无关，好的年头，种的粮食仅仅够填饱肚子。靠田吃饭的东塘村民，实际是靠天吃饭。即使是最好的年头，亩产至多也就500斤。而在其他地区，依靠机械科学种植，亩产千斤早已不稀奇。可是东塘村的村民大多只上过小学和初中，不少人连科学种田"听都没听过"。在东塘，机械化种植几乎是空白，拖拉机、肥料这些新东西，在缺乏文化技术知识的大多村民眼里实在多余，既不会捣鼓也不想用。

2010年以前，村民黎学贵的房子里家徒四壁，没有日历，没有时钟。几乎是文盲的黎学贵，这样的生活延续多年。早晨他跟着邻居下地，晚上跟着大家收工。家里的三个孩子成为黎学贵的负担。可自家的土地却没有多少，为了提高产出，黎学贵只能一地两用，割完水稻后，立刻种上番薯。曾经有技术员告诉村民，应该如何科学施种才能提高产量，但他和邻居却怎么也记不住，更学不会。

周末，两个读书的孩子必须回家，因为田里需要他们，但家里却没有多余的床，两个孩子只能去邻居家借住。然而就是这样耗尽心力地去维护这一亩三分田，耗时耗力，甚至包括对生活的热情，都花费在这里。因为，这里能让一家人吃上饭，遇上好的年头甚至可以吃饱饭。不幸的是，几乎没有家庭能从口粮中省出可供变现的余粮。有人曾试着种花生、辣椒，但都"只有热情，不懂技术"，忙活了一年甚至还要赔钱。

无法融入的外乡世界

上世纪90年代，数以百万计的务工人员涌入珠三角，这个遍地是金的寻梦天堂。

东塘人也加入了务工大军。滚滚车轮，载着一批批怀有赚钱养家梦的人走出东塘。然而，幸运之神似乎有意躲着他们——村民从未听说谁在外面赚了钱，走出去的人很快又都回到村里。

十多年过去了，除了通向村里的黄土路铺上了水泥，村民说其他没有任何改变。

东塘村郑鑫一家，四年前买的红砖，现在还堆在角落，早已布满青苔。2006年，郑家住了几十年的茅草屋已破败不堪。外面下雨，屋里涨大水。这年的一场大雨后，茅屋遭遇灭顶之灾，坍塌了大半。

就在同一年，郑鑫22岁的儿子初三毕业，在朋友介绍下去了广州打工。一家人认为老大去了大城市闯，生活就有了依靠，于是决定盖房。从亲戚那里借的2万盖房钱很快就花完了，但在广州的儿子却连饭都吃不饱。因为听不懂普通话，更不懂技术，他只好跟着老乡捡破烂。盖房梦被迫中断，原来的草房亦不复存在。无奈之下，他们搬进附近的树林，用树枝搭起两个"木帐篷"。小的给老母亲住，郑鑫和老婆住在大帐篷里。工作了四年的郑家老大，现在每个月工资仅800元。在电话里，他告诉奶奶，外面太苦，他想回家种田。

村里的中年人，年轻时也和郑家老大一样，曾走出东塘，到珠三角或邻近省份打工，但顶多做三年就回来了。究其原因还是东塘人文化程度不高，一口地道的"雷州普通话"，浓重的乡音让人难以理解。沟通不畅自然也消磨了晋升的通道。

满口的"雷普"（雷州普通话）源自东塘小学。当年的学校课堂上，老师用一字一顿的普通话教孩子学拼音，转身喝道："安静！"此时，普通话又变成雷州方言。这是2010年以前的景象，当时301名学生全部来自本村，老师也都是本地人，他们也无奈，村里有电视的家庭不超过1/20，互联网更是新鲜事物，土生土长的老师很少接触到外面的世界。

很多教师是小学毕业后就留校任教，教书多年后通过进修才拿到文凭，早就错过了学普通话的最佳时期。"雷州普通话"就这样代代相传。表面上看，东塘"小升初"的入学率达到100%。农村孩子上学晚，8岁上一年级"还算早"，进入初中时大部分都超过16岁。

一批批说着纯正"雷州普通话"的大龄初中生，走出家门，重拾父辈之路。现实再多的困难，也阻挡不住他们对外面世界的渴望。一批批走出去的东塘人，在外艰难闯荡一两年后，含泪而归。接过父辈的锄头，结婚生子，终其贫穷而平凡的一生。

"中国制造2025"
与教育扶贫

　　2014年12月，"中国制造2025"这一概念被首次提出。4个月后，2015年3月5日，李克强在全国两会上作《政府工作报告》时首次提出"中国制造2025"的宏大计划。"中国制造2025"是中国政府实施制造强国战略第一个十年的行动纲领。第一步，到2025年迈入制造强国行列；第二步，到2035年中国制造业整体达到世界制造强国阵营中等水平；第三步，到新中国成立一百年时，综合实力进入世界制造强国前列。

　　"中国制造2025"这样的制造业大升级任务要完成，优质的职业人才教育是不可或缺的。随着城市化进程推进，广东大量流动人口就有成为优质产业工人的潜力，珠三角中国制造业两大门户地区，需要大量优质产业工人。可贫困阻挡了山区流动人口学习知识、培训技能的道路。东塘村的教育现状也反映了广东教育扶贫的难题：教育基础设施建设投入不足，师资力量不均衡，毕业生出路不明朗。

　　对于这些贫困家庭和他们的孩子，接济衣物、粮食和解决住房等，也许能果腹暖身，但只是除一时之困，并非长久之计。扶贫须先扶智。大山里的居民其实知道，要想富，得走出去；要想走出去，要多读几年书。学好普通话，提高文化素质，才能在"人"这个问题上确保扶贫效果。

2009年12月，深圳坪山新区与包括东塘村在内的东里镇四村结成帮扶伙伴。不懂普通话，职业技能无法提高？东塘村贫困户中有劳动力198人，深圳坪山新区按照"培训一人、就业一人、脱贫一户"的原则，安排他们免费参加技能培训，有组织、有目的地引导其到新区务工，努力掌握技术和经验，为未来回乡创业推进集体脱贫做准备。

与此同时，村道一旁的东塘小学变了模样，坪山新区投入3.36万元建设的一栋钢筋混凝土结构的公厕赫然挺立在东塘小学的西南角，同期建设的还有一座垃圾池，彻底解决了该校300多名师生入厕难的问题，显著地改善了学校的卫生环境。

在村外，有陌生人偶遇几个骑车嬉闹的村里小孩儿，原以为他们就像一路上遇到的大人们一样，听不懂普通话。岂料，突然一个小男孩用普通话上前问道："你要去哪儿？"

治贫先治愚

2015年10月16日，在2015减贫与发展高层论坛上，来自广东顺德的碧桂园创始人杨国强被授予"中国消除贫困奖（创新奖）"，他开启了教育扶贫领域"政社互动"帮扶的范本。作为地产大亨，杨国强和他的女儿杨惠妍曾登顶"福布斯"中国财富富豪榜，改革开放将近40年，碧桂园从无到有，地产项目遍布中国一、二、三线城市。

2010年以来，杨国强父女和碧桂园6年间捐赠超过13亿元用于广东扶贫济困事业。此前捐赠的超过8亿元，用于在清远、肇庆、广州等地推进树山村绿色产业扶贫、怀集县扶贫、梯面镇扶贫、送技术技能下乡培训、广东碧桂园职业学院、滴灌精准扶贫等六大项目。

出生于广东顺德一个贫困农民家庭的杨国强，17岁前几乎没穿过鞋。他从不曾忘记，在他因家贫不得不辍学之际，政府不仅免了他每学期7元学费，还给予2元助学金，让他完成了高中学业。他深切感受到教育对于彻底脱贫的积极意义，事业有成后，他开始踏上教育扶贫之路。

多年以后，当他回忆起年少奋斗的时光时，觉得那应该是追求知识的渴望。杨国强说，在碧桂园集团的财务总监，是他同宗族的兄弟，两人同时得了国家2元钱补贴，免了7元钱学费。两人用4元钱去废品收购站买了一堆书，甚至包括大学课本。

1997年，杨国强捐资100万元匿名设立"仲明奖学金"资助贫困大学生，18年中不断增加捐助，先后有8000多名学子受惠；2002年，杨国强出资2.6亿元创办了国华纪念中学，免费招收家庭贫困、成绩优秀的学生，提供助学金直至学生完成大学、硕士、博士所有阶段的学业；2013年，杨国强又出资3.5亿元创办广东碧桂园职业学院，所有入读学生不仅免除一切费用，还领取日常生活补贴。广东碧桂园职业学院现在是广东典型的职业教育扶贫项目。

目前，这所全免费的大专学校，接收了672名贫困学生。经过两年招生，其中大部分为广东籍贫困学生。

2012年，在清远市佛冈县水头镇，杨国强探索出了另外一种教育扶贫方式，他将职业教育的课堂搬到了村子里，开展"送技术技能下乡培训项目"。该项目对全镇16~60周岁适龄劳动力，开展免费的技术技能培训，还联系用工单位，帮助受训农民找工作。三年来，该项目免费培训16469人，其中8150人取得叉车、电工、家政育婴师等9种职业资格证书，通过推荐就业，3828人进城就业。

杨国强认为，学院一方面要系统培养高素质技术技能型人才；另一方面要以学院的精英式培养来改变社会对高职的看法，从而让更多学子喜欢读高职，进而改良中国高等教育结构。

来自人社部的一项统计也验证了杨国强的说法，中国2.25亿第二产业就业人员中，技能劳动者总量仅为1.19亿人，仅制造业高级技工一项的缺口就高达400余万人，高级技能人才的供需矛盾十分严重，从而阻碍了企业的技术升级。2015年"两会"上，身为全国政协委员的杨国强联合三位全国政协委员，提交了一份《关于鼓励和引导民营企业积极参与教育扶贫的提案》。

重视职教扶贫这一思路得到了国家层面的认可。国务院发布规定，对构建现代职业教育体系提出了明确的目标要求。

教育扶贫投入大、环节多、时间长，坚持不易，但效果显著，可以做到"培养一人，脱贫一户"，彻底阻断贫困代际传递，实现个人、家庭、社会的共赢。18年的教育扶贫，4万多名受助者摆脱了贫困，杨国强说："我所拥有的财富只是社会交给我保管的，有了能力帮助别人是很自然和正常的，我只是尽自己本分而已。我始终觉得，人的素质是最重要的，教育扶贫就是'授人以渔'。"

医疗扶贫：
消除60万人
贫困之源

疾病挡住了致富的脚步

　　健康和卫生在减少甚至消除贫困中的地位尤为重要。世界卫生组织总干事陈冯富珍在2015减贫与发展高层论坛上致辞时指出，卫生、健康与贫困至少在三方面都是紧密联系的。贫困会影响人们的健康，包括那些贫困的、不健康的、不卫生的环境，失业，缺乏营养以及使用药物或者烟草，这些都对精神和身体的健康发起挑战。更好的健康使得人们能够更容易摆脱贫困。

　　在广东176.5万相对贫困人口中，因病致贫比例达到36.2%。这意味着，疾病已成为横亘在广东超过60万人脱贫路上最大的"拦路虎"。病倒一个人就塌下一个家。如何让农民病有所医，是广东扶贫中面临的一大难题。

　　人均仅四分田地，养不活一家老小，这是粤东梅州溪口村的现实。人多地少，唯一的解决方案就是"走出大山，外出务工"。溪口人早就知道脱贫致富的出路。但并不是所有溪口人都能走出大山，去到县城，再去到更远的珠三角。当地很多家庭，其成员因病丧失了劳动能力，没有富余的劳力向山外输出——病魔就如藤蔓，拴住了他们迈出大山、脱贫致富的脚步。

疾病面前，这些家庭余下的一两个劳动力，显得形只影单。溪口村地处广东省梅州市大埔县青溪镇西部。2010年前，溪口村总人口1748人，其中年收入1500元以下的贫困家庭181户，贫困人口726人。全村水田242亩，人均仅四分田地，绝大部分人不得不外出务工。

在外闯荡30年后，刘长喜回到溪口，身无长物，332省道旁的一间土坯民房是他的全部。他努力了半生，试图改变命运，但到最后，他还是败给了疾病。

刘长喜是改革开放以后，当地最早外出务工的那批人之一。1977年，刘长喜离开溪口，因为只有小学文化，进不了国营厂矿，只能四处奔走，出卖劳力。刘长喜经人介绍，去了广东省惠州市龙门县，受雇于当地人，为其照看山上的经济作物。10多年后，已经50多岁的刘长喜才终于结婚，妻子小他15岁，他的妻子有过一次婚姻经历，是一名寡妇，还患有癫痫。

婚姻，让刘长喜如浮萍般的命运有了归属，但也让他渐有起色的生活重新晦暗。婚后，妻子常常犯病，为了给老婆治病，刘长喜四处寻医问药。20世纪90年代初，"新农合"还没有普及，老婆的医疗费、四处奔走的路费似沉重的负担，令刘长喜窒息。

2010年，76岁的刘长喜一生与贫病纠缠，41岁的丁瑞辉步其后尘。2006年，丁瑞辉的妻子因病去世，为了照顾年迈的双亲和三个没成年的女儿，老丁终止了打工生涯，回归了农民身份。妻子去世前，丁家的生活有了起色，夫妻二人还回乡盖了两间新砖房，但给妻子治病，老丁欠下了几万元的债务，四年后，钱还没还清。

丁家目前六口人，只有三亩多田地。农忙后，老丁还要去茶阳镇、青溪镇做临工。临工收入不定，老丁手头很少有余钱，他一个劳力要供养六口人，给父母治病要花钱，大女儿读中学需要生活费。

溪口村只是广东贫困山区因为疾病而导致贫困的一部分人的缩影。一部分外出人员的确脱贫了，但有些人因为没文化，出去没什么好工作，赚钱也不易。扶贫干部李庆祥认为，目前，大部分贫困山区的青壮年大部分都是初中毕业，完成了义务教育，就不读书了，初中学历，到外面也只能做最底层的活。

因病致贫，一方面是因为农民家庭经济基础薄弱，无力负担医疗费用。另一方面则是因为疾病夺走了家庭成员的劳动能力，一个家庭只有壮年男性一个劳动力，导致家庭跌入贫困线。

李庆祥说，家庭成员因病丧失劳动力，甚至死亡，最后导致家境每况愈下，此类家庭占到贫困家庭里的绝大多数。而一些家庭好不容易脱贫，却又因病返贫，是困扰山区扶贫的难题。

所有的致贫原因最后串联成一条线索：缺少田地，农民难以靠传统农业致富，不得已，外出务工——囿于文化水平低，务工人员工资收入也低，家庭徘徊于穷苦之境——一些家庭为了治病导致经济负担增加，成员丧失劳动力（甚至死亡），这使得这些家庭成了最穷的那批人。

农村医疗的一波三折

在7年前，刘长喜所在的一个生产队300多人，只配有一间卫生院，卫生院的医生还多是大专、中专学历，要他们包治百病不可能，这是很多贫困山区医疗条件的现状。

说是家医院，却治不了老百姓的病，卫生院的院长涂启智谈起七八年前的窘境也很无奈，他当时手下只有10名医生、3名护士。

除了人少，卫生院的设施也很简陋，当时最先进的设备也只是一台黑白B超。老医生退休，卫生院一直找不到能顶上的医生。涂启智以前为此常常去大埔县卫生局要人，可他也自知，招到医生的可能性有限，"主要是卫生院小，工资低，没有吸引力"。

作为院长，老涂当时每月的工资是1500多元，他手下的医生，大专学历的月工资700多元，中专学历的月工资600多元。

由于乡镇卫生院的工资与城市医院的工资差距大，有经验的医生大量外流，到卫生院看病的群众也是逐年减少。

作为一名基层医务人员，农民看病难，涂启智感同身受。

目前，中国的基本医保主要分为三种，分别是职工医保、城镇居民医保、新农合。这其中，城镇居民医保由财政和城镇居民缴费，由人社部门管理；新农合由财政和农民缴费，由卫计部门管理。

在20世纪70年代，中国农村合作医疗制度与农村的县、乡、村三级医疗保健制度、赤脚医生一起成为解决我国广大农村缺医少药问题，保障人民群众健康的农村医疗"三大法宝"，农村合作医疗模式被世界卫生组织和世界银行盛赞为"以最少投入获得最大健康收益的模式"，并被作为样板向第三世界国家推广。1978年合作医疗写入《中华人民共和国宪法》，到农村生产责任制改革之前的1978年，全国农村合作医疗覆盖率达到80%～90%。

进入20世纪80年代，全国农村实行家庭联产承包责任制，人民公社被取消，生产大队也随之解体，农村集体经济迅速萎缩，合作医疗制度快速走向解体，绝大部分村卫生室、合作医疗站变成了乡村医生的私人诊所，农民缺医少药的现象再次出现。据调查，合作医疗覆盖率由1980年68.8%骤降到1983年的20%以下。据1985年的统计调查，全国实行合作医疗的行政村由过去的90%降到了5%。在20世纪90年代，我国政府推行"民办公助，自愿参加"的政策，两度试图重建农村合作医疗，但在制度设计上没有明确社会保障国家主体责任的定位，恢复和建立的工作都没有收到预期的成效。有一组数据可以说明当时农村合作医疗的窘境，国家财政卫生事业费用中用于农村合作医疗的补助费1979年是1亿元，1992年下降到3500万元，仅占卫生事业费用的0.36%。

本世纪初，伴随着城乡发展不协调矛盾的日益突出，2002年10月中国重新开启了农村合作医疗制度的建设工作，并把过去的农村合作医疗制度称之为新型农村合作医疗制度。新农合除了针对日常门诊和住院，大病保险也纳入范畴。以广州市为例，如今，农村居民只要缴纳100元/年的新农合费用，各级政府就会补贴340元/年，农村居民就可以享受门诊就医50%，住院治疗70%的报销额度。如果发生重大疾病，在医保报销之后，个人自付部分还可以享受50%以上的报销。报销最高限额为15万元一年。

2016年年初，广东实现了农村和城镇人口两种医保制度相整合。广东城乡医保并轨后，各地医保定点的医疗机构、医保药品的目录，都明显扩大。尤其对不少新农合参保人来说，整合后医保用药范围成倍增长。广东城乡医保并轨后，城乡居民统一使用基本医保药品目录，农民的可报销药品种类分别从1100种、1083种、918种扩大到2400种、2450种、2100种，医保用药的范围增加1倍多。

医疗扶贫：
"一条龙"健康扶贫到家

　　除了加强新农合医保，广东也在利用新制度和新技术来解决医疗扶贫问题。

　　连南地区是广东省贫困落后地区，医疗卫生水平与全省平均水平有较大的差距。此前当地曾有三家大型医院，但由于医疗技术与医疗环境水平有限，三家医院都不能吸引病人，不少当地人会到邻县连州和连山看病，估计比例达到40%以上。如何将纷纷赶赴外地治病的病人留在本地？

　　广东药学院相关负责人说，广东药学院帮扶性托管连南人民医院，并不是出于商业目的，更多的是公益性、社会责任的担当。而在托管之后，该院实行去行政化的法人代表管理模式，成立了负责医院管理决策的董事会和监督董事会的监事会。医院的所有职务都去行政化，取消行政级别，医院的领导班子成员由董事会任命。广东药学院派出的管理团队以及技术骨干也极大提高了连南医院的水平。

　　除了新农合制度和医疗下沉以外，新技术也为医疗扶贫难题提出解决方案。91岁高龄的梁保在6年前中风了，半身瘫痪的他活动范围就是十几平方米大小的屋子，就连想在家门口晒太阳都难，更不要说上医院了。2016年10月16日，由广东省第二人民医院阳山医院集团全体党员及广东省网络医院推出的阳山县家庭医生团队，专程赶到梁保所在的清远市阳山县范村，与他签约，并在未来提供免费的精准治疗。这是省第二人民医院阳山医院集团对口帮扶推出的新福利。

广东省扶贫办2016年8月公布的数据显示，全省相对贫困户主要致贫原因前3位分别是因病（36.2%）、缺劳力（23.3%）、因残（19.9%）。清远市阳山县是贫困山区的一个缩影。阳山一共有159个村，广东省网络医院院长周其如和下属工作人员逐村筛查出了2000多户"因病致贫、因病返贫"的贫困户。

为了让优质医疗资源下沉至基层，提升基层乡村的医疗卫生服务能力，省第二人民医院阳山医院集团提出利用"互联网+大众医疗"技术来进行医疗扶贫。

专家们发现，在阳山，像梁保一样不能出远门看病的居民有很多，必须提供上门服务。广东省网络医院线上线下的健康管理团队，开始对他们进行"一条龙"的健康管理。

家庭医生团队由村医、镇卫生院公卫医生、广东省网络医院医生、省第二人民医院阳山医院集团党员及专家组成。签约后，医生将为签约家庭建立完善居民健康档案、更新健康档案内容。此外，还将提供老、幼、妇和重大疾病、慢性疾病的追踪服务和省、县、镇、村4级医疗机构的资源共享等个性化的优惠服务。

阳山这2000多户"因病致贫、因病返贫"的贫困户都将与家庭医生团队签约。两年内使这些贫困户家中的患病人群全部得到免费的精准治疗，同步对他们进行健康管理，从根本上改善他们的生活质量，使其脱贫致富。

如今刘长喜已经加入了新农合，随着大病保险的覆盖，他妻子的疾病报销比例大幅提高，他的家庭困境得到了缓解。与此同时，随着医疗力量的下沉，刘长喜所在的大队迎来了两名科班出身的社区医生，刘长喜等不用再赶到十几公里外的县城看病问诊了。

交通扶贫：
"修条好路给农村既是出路也是活路"

大动脉通了毛细血管却没通

　　改革开放将近40年，在致富路上农民悟出了许多道理，其中最为显著的是"要致富、先修路，富不富、先看路"，可见农村公路在我国经济发展中的重要地位和作用。交通是制约经济发展的瓶颈，而农村公路畅通与否又是农村经济发展的关键。

　　广东，作为中国改革开放春风最早吹过的省份，在交通运输等基础设施建设上一直领先于全国。到2015年年底，广东高速公路通车里程达到7018公里，在全国率先突破7000公里，继续保持领先水平。实现全省"县县通高速"目标，出省通道达到17条，实现与陆路相邻省份开通3条以上出省通道；粤东西北地区高速公路网络也得到明显改善，通车里程达到3282公里，外通内连、协调均衡的高速公路骨干网络基本形成。一系列数字反映，广东的道路设施投入并不少，成果也不小。可道路建设多集中在珠三角等经济发达区域，对于粤东西北等山区，交通基础设施的欠账却仍有不少。

　　广东省河源市杨梅村曾经有很多大龄青年因交通闭塞娶不到媳妇，"小伙子长得都很好，有什么办法呢？"对于贫穷的肇因，村民们无不指出，"路太烂"。

出村难，成为杨梅人最深刻的记忆。早些年，杨梅人到河源市区办事。早上7时30分出发，走山路2小时到锡场镇码头，再坐船摆渡，中午12时30分才能抵达河源，下午万一没办成事，只能花钱住旅馆。

村民天天都盼着修好路

　　村民詹石源，曾在2001年种过几十亩果树。"因为这条破山路，老板不愿来收，来了还不断压价，外面卖一元，这里只卖三五毛。"因交通不便，几乎所有村民每次种养都亏本。不管青菜还是水果，外面收货的车都要在东面7公里的山外等。杨梅村有一台部队退役下来的烂炮车，"只有它能把货从烂泥路中运出去"。加上人工过车费、雇车费及等待的费用，村民们运货每车的成本为150~200元。

　　2008年，锡场镇禾石坑村一个农民在库区成功培育灵芝，收入可观，随后灵芝被推广至全镇，东源县甚至将锡场镇定为"灵芝专业镇"。灵芝培育，一夜间似乎成了杨梅村脱贫的灵丹妙药。"第一年种的人赚了几千元，第二年村民们一拥而上，十多户培育面积达12亩。"2009年村民李业生用东风卡车运了6大车木头，光种子就花了6000元，培育了2500多斤灵芝。

　　可刺痛杨梅人是，到了5月份木桩里种子全部发黑，一堆堆蒸好、培上种子的木头只能用来烧火。"到现在还搞不清原因，很多人说是感染了，但没有专家愿意进山指导我们。"

2007年经过争取，村东侧10.5公里镇通村公路被修通。但西侧7公里的经济路，村民争取了多次始终没有立项。国家扶贫开发领导小组的调研人员，对东部省份的扶贫开发工作做了调查，调研人员发现，广东贫困地区基础设施欠账较大，与产业发展需要非常不适应，改善贫困人口的生产生活条件仍然是一项繁重的任务。

直到2012年，帮扶单位才在杨梅村实现了村西侧7公里经济路项目的立项审批，筹资240余万元，准备让这条经济路在当年年底修通。

修条好路既是出路也是活路

　　泗水村是上一轮（2013—2015年）"双到"扶贫中的被帮扶村庄，已顺利脱贫。省人大代表、梅州市平远县泗水镇泗水村党支部书记、村委会主任王满秀介绍，从上一轮"双到"扶贫得出的经验是，贫困村民要想脱贫致富，必须先把村里的道路修好。泗水村村民主要是种蔬菜、种树。没有路，客商进不来，东西运不出去，只能烂在地里。泗水村的情况在贫困村中普遍存在，道路等基础设施不完善，是造成贫困的一个重要因素。不少贫困村与泗水村类似，并不是缺乏资源或产业，只是受限于交通闭塞、道路不畅等原因，优质的农产品难以对外销售，良好的旅游资源无法得到开发和推介。农民不出去、企业进不来，天然有机的农产品烂在了地里，秀丽宜人的自然风光掩埋在了深山，农民坐拥丰富的自然资源，却无法进行开发利用，日子越过越贫困。

　　加快农村经济发展，必须加大农村公路建设，加强农村公路管理，改善交通运输环境，为农村产业结构调整和商品流通铺平道路，促进农民增收致富。

　　广东要在2018年率先全面建成小康社会，脱贫攻坚是必须取胜的关键战役。抓好农村基础设施建设作为精准扶贫精准脱贫的八项工程之一，不仅要把路修通，而且要构建互相串联、有效贯通的交通体系，从而发展产业、盘活资源、增加收入，增强贫困村的"造血功能"。

广东省交通厅制订计划，到2018年，在县县通高速公路基础上，进一步完善贫困地区高速公路网络。以县乡公路路面改造为重点，加强贫困地区县乡道建设。

全国人大代表，清远连南瑶族自治县寨岗镇山联村党支部书记、村委会主任何桂芳所在的村曾因交通滞后，信息闭塞，发展落后，被当地人称为连南的"西伯利亚"。多年来，在何桂芳的多方呼吁下，村里的路通了，电通了，发展加快，村民生活逐渐改善。他认为，广东集中力量改善贫困地区的生产生活条件，就是要补齐农村发展短板。"要修条好路给农村。对农民来讲，这是出路，也是活路。"全国人大代表、广东中山纪念中学原校长贺优琳说。

金融扶贫：
加速脱贫之路

农业"缺钱"之痛：
春耕资金缺口大

　　说起广东的贫困地区，很多人都以为在粤东西北地区，其实在珠三角地区也有贫困存在。金坑村位于"江门五邑"之一的恩平东成镇，面积10.4平方公里，包括5个自然村，471户，总人口1499人。耕地2300亩，主要以附加值低的水稻种植为主，村人均年收入3100元左右。村民除出国做生意外，也有部分到恩平、江门、中山、广州等地打工。

　　资金是制约金坑村农业发展的主要问题之一。

　　1995年，恩平爆发因高息揽储带来的银行挤兑危机，银行接连倒闭，十余年时间内当地金融机构的发展一度非常萧条。当地商业银行大幅收缩服务网点，由发生风险前的266个减少到现在的43个。

　　而在农村地区，由于恩平城乡信用社已经撤销，金融服务只能依靠邮政储蓄银行得以维系，其他金融机构要么没有农业金融服务，要么"只存不贷"。相关数据显示，截至2007年底当地所有的农业贷款余额仅有48万元，仅占江门地区农业贷款总额的0.03%。

　　金坑村只是广东广大贫困农村的一个缩影。1998年以来，金融对"三农"的支持基本空白。最基本的水稻种植方面，也缺乏资金支持。据恩平市农业局测算，2006年恩平全市春耕资金需求约5040万元，农民自有资金约1180万元，资金缺口高达3860万元。

农业保险缺位:
金融风险农民独担

"恩平地处珠三角,交通便利,市场大,种养业按说很有市场。"恩平市农业局副局长冯浪其说,养殖等不但需要技术、资金,农业保险也要跟上。

但农业保险迟迟不能跟上。据了解,从2006年开始,恩平市保险业界对效益相对低下的农业项目涉入较少,尝试性开办的个别农业险种(水果种植),由于长期亏损,目前已基本停止办理。农业保险缺失,不能有效分散农业风险,而相应的风险补偿机制又未建立,进一步制约着金融机构对农村建设的投入,形成恶性循环。

2006年,乡村银行的创办者,被誉为"穷人的银行家"的尤努斯教授凭此获得诺贝尔和平奖。消息使中国备受鼓舞,开放农村金融市场的改革新政由此酝酿。

2006年12月,银监会出台政策首次允许产业资本和民间资本到农村地区新设银行,并提出要在农村增设村镇银行、贷款公司和农村资金互助社等三类金融机构,被金融业界称作第四轮中国农村金融改革破冰之举。

"小额贷款难,这在全国农村来说具有一定的普遍性。"中国社会科学院农村发展研究所研究员张元红表示，盈利作为银行主要的营业目标，不断加强成本结算，在收缩过于分散的农村网点的同时将贷款额度的审批权开始上收，目前县以下的营业网点基本上没有审批贷款的权力。

让金融重返农村

事实上，金融服务力度在农村的的不足已引起各方的重视。

2009年，广东有60多个零银行业金融机构网点的乡镇，主要分布在粤东、粤西和粤北经济不发达、金融业规模比较小的区域。2010—2013年，广东通过逐步推进新型农村金融机构试点类型和范围、鼓励商业银行和农村信用社增设机构网点等方式，才逐步填补了零银行业金融机构网点乡镇的空白。

村镇银行的模式也被引入中国，在小范围内进行试点。2007年底，广东正式开始筹划新型农村金融机构试点工作。恩平和乳源被选定为广东的首批试点地区。2009年3月，汇丰恩平村镇银行正式开业，引入"公司+农户"的小额信贷业务：围绕当地较大的农业龙头企业，向与其长年发生业务往来的农户和经销商提供相应的贷款，重点支持恩平农村居民、城镇居民、农村小微企业和农业中小企业金融的需求。

为发展"三农"，中国目前正推出系列政策：鼓励大型商业股份制银行下乡，主动向农民提供小额贷款，帮助发展生产；在条件成熟的发达地区，增加营业网点，方便农民办理贷款业务；进行新型农村金融体制的创新，成立农村户主组织和小额贷款公司，帮助农民解决贷款难的问题。

一些贫困地区缺乏有效的经济增长模式和商业模式，金融资本难以有效进入，难以形成可持续性。面对担保难、抵押物不足、贷款主体不合格等困扰贫困地区脱贫的"老大难"问题，广东银行业围绕农村综合改革，创新配套金融产品，结合农民"融资难"、农村"金融贫血"等"症结"开出多元化"药方"。

为了破解担保难的问题，广东清远银行业针对800余户已确权的土地承包经营权，创新推出了"流转贷"产品。"在农村土地确权登记颁证的基础上，农民可以根据自身需要，向农业银行申请贷款，把土地资源转化为贷款资金。"中国农业银行广东清远分行副行长李亮表示。

广东英德市农村信用合作社了解当地情况之后，创新推出"农改贷"产品，适度放宽了对借款主体必须经工商部门注册登记的限制，向耕地分散的英德市石牯塘镇萤火村叶屋村经济合作社授信200万元，支持其开展土地流转，提高土地利用效率。

为实现精准扶贫，广东省委推行"驻村帮扶+建档立卡"模式，在全省范围内积极开展扶贫"双到"工作，即"规划到户、责任到人"，驻村帮扶，定村定户，定责定人，一定3年，限期脱贫。

该模式为建档立卡贫困户提供专门的扶贫小额信贷，确保资金投放到生产，投放到就业。广东银监局鼓励银行业金融机构在准确评定贫困户信用等级和还款能力的基础上，向有贷款意愿、有就业创业潜质、有技能素质的建档立卡贫困户提供5万元以下、3年以内的信用贷款，满足其生产、创业、就业、搬迁安置等各类贷款需求，同时对扶贫小额信贷实行利率优惠。

技术反哺
扶贫路

贫困户手机淘宝卖圣女果

2016年春节前，"超级寒潮"南下，广东大部分地区遭到冰雪袭击，长年"看天吃饭"的农产品大量减产。然而，在湛江、清远连州等地，部分贫困村农民却并未因为减产而收入大减，有些甚至获得了比往年更好的收入。带来这种变化的是如今为广东各地扶贫干部们所津津乐道、广泛传播的"电商扶贫""移动互联网扶贫"。

春节刚过，塘头村的贫困村民罗儒廷已经接到了几箱圣女果的订单，正准备到田间收果发货。因为节前的寒潮，田间的圣女果种苗有些已经干枯。"今年挂果不多，早上摘，下午就发货，用班车送到广州。"罗儒廷随手在田间摘下几把微微泛红的圣女果，"这种七八成熟的就可以摘了，这样待果子在路上自然熟透，送到买家手中刚刚好"。

罗儒廷种的圣女果品种叫做"千禧"。"千禧"品种是2014年由广州驻湛江扶贫干部通过电商平台上获取的信息，从海南引进。正是"千禧"的引进，改变了塘头村的圣女果广种薄收又没有好价钱的窘境。

2013年之前，罗儒廷种的几亩"万福"圣女果，由于被批发商收购压价，收成仅能勉强维持妻子的药钱和孩子的学费。村党支部委员、村民罗祝说："以前圣女果的收购价一斤大概只有5毛钱，现在千禧的收购价至少都要1块起，除去种子、肥料、人工费，每亩果子的利润能有1.5万元。"

曾经对智能手机一窍不通的罗儒廷，如今已经熟悉了电商的运作，负责接塘头村的订单，并组织货源发货。他打开手机展示"湛江驻村人扶贫专营店"的微店页面，上面的农产品琳琅满目。

"田里信号不好，我们通常都去村委会的电脑上查看订单。"罗儒廷称，村委会现在只有一台电脑，正准备用市里的财政专项拨款采购几台新的电脑。

他还颇为自豪地说："我们的圣女果在上面是卖得最好的，还有北京、天津、上海的订单。"如今，塘头村圣女果的订单来源已经覆盖整个珠三角。接到订单后，罗儒廷就会组织收购，用快递或班车发出去。仅2015年12月，他就接到了十几笔大订单，跟了四趟车送货到广州。

岑宇铿是广州驻湛江雷州塘头村的扶贫干部，"农产品电商"的发起人。在塘头村民眼中，"这个个子不高、年纪不大、戴着眼镜、斯斯文文的广州小伙子，很能干"！在岑宇铿看来，塘头村的土地以沙地为主，比较贫瘠，地少人多，农业排灌设施差。303户村民中，就有105户贫困户，脱贫任务非常重。

"我们到村里后，发现最大的问题，就是农民无法了解市场的信息，一直都是靠原有的种植技术去种植农产品，包括圣女果。"岑宇铿说，此前圣女果苗和种子都是收购商提供的，收购商不仅压价严重，"还会扣除10%的烂果率的钱"。"即使农民有一定的利润空间，但不足以让他们脱贫致富。"

　　他想到了已经在全国大城市中发展得轰轰烈烈的移动互联网。2014年3月25日，淘宝上的"塘头村扶贫农产品专营店"正式上线，塘头村成为最早"试水"电商扶贫的地方。

　　据中国工信部通报，2016年中国移动电话用户规模达到12.8亿，移动互联网用户总数达9.8亿户。如今移动互联网已深刻影响人们的生活。

　　在美国上市的阿里巴巴公司所拥有的淘宝网是中国深受欢迎的网购零售平台，目前拥有近5亿的注册用户，每天有超过6000万的固定访客，同时每天的在线商品数已经超过了8亿件，平均每分钟售出4.8万件商品。而腾讯公司所属的微信日活跃用户量超过了6.7亿人次。目前，在中国大中型城市，人们出门可以不用携带现金和信用卡，餐饮、服装、超市等消费场所几乎都与互联网支付接轨。甚至连医院、出租车、停车场和高速公路都能用手机完成付费。

　　"村里的农民和贫困户开始不理解，他们认为电商很虚，不能够真的帮到他们。"为了让村民信任"电商"，岑宇铿找到了当地最大的收购商，并与其合作，先在淘宝店上帮贫困户卖圣女果。结果，仅2014年上半年，就帮助农户销售"万福"圣女果达3万多斤。与此同时，岑宇铿等人在电商平台上了解到，海南有一种叫"千禧"的圣女果，国内少有地方种植，价值更高。于是，驻村干部从海南买来了嫁接苗，开出了100亩的"千禧"基地，并邀请海南的专家对在基地里务工的贫困户进行技术培训。

　　2015年元旦后，"千禧"圣女果大量上市，并在淘宝店上热卖，吸引了大量买家。2015年"千禧"基地营收超过200万元，单是支付给贫困户农民采摘、包装等劳务工资就超过70万元。2016年1月份，基地圣女果上市，田头收购价达到了每市斤7.5元。2015年10

月起，塘头村"千禧"种植面积已经从100亩，变成了350亩，几乎所有村民都种起了"千禧"品种。

早在2014年10月，塘头村的农产品电商经验被广州驻湛江扶贫工作队推广到了整个湛江的95个贫困村，淘宝店的名字也改成了"湛江驻村人扶贫专营店"。在"湛江驻村人扶贫专营店"上，95个村的农产品均可在上面展示、销售，圣女果、香瓜、黑米、红米、黑山羊、火龙果以及海产品等应有尽有。

如今，整个雷州半岛的农民都跟着种起了"千禧"圣女果，面积超过3000亩。通过电商扶贫，扶贫干部还与村民们一起建立了青枣、香瓜、火龙果基地，种植面积超过6000亩。除此之外，他们还引入了黑米、红米、东方一号密瓜等优质农产品，生产广受追捧的芝麻花生油。

截至2016年2月底，通过电商平台对接珠三角、长三角和京津冀等市场，湛江地区贫困户各类农产品线上线下销售额早已突破千万元。广州驻湛扶贫工作队还建立起了"电商平台+种植仓储加工产业基地+合作社+农户"的模式。这为当地贫困村建立稳定脱贫长效机制提供了很好的平台，据统计，电商扶贫惠及湛江地区贫困户达3万户。

如今，罗儒廷、罗祝等塘头村的村民已经熟悉了网上销售农产品的流程，而三年来的"电商扶贫"，已经在湛江95个贫困村产生了巨大的"电商效应"。驻村干部们还帮助村民们成立了一个由12户农户组成的农民专业合作社，已经能够带动88户贫困户，并以此带动其他88户贫困户脱贫。

2015年5月至8月，岑宇铿受国务院全国贫困地区干部深圳培训基地邀请，先后为西藏、云南、江西、河南、湖南、湖北及广东七个省、自治区的扶贫干部讲授电商扶贫。在岑宇铿看来，电商扶贫实际上只是"互联网+农业"的一个探索，由国家层面推进才可以真正解决贫困地区农产品的销售。

他认为，官方应尽快建立农业大数据库，不仅对农业企业开放，更要对普通农民开放。"比如气候的大数据、农产品价格的大数据、地域性的产品的对比、种子商出售种子的数据等等，大的电商平台都可以开放自己的数据库给农民。如果实在不行，那就由政府来购买这些数据，并对农民开放。"

"村长大米"入住苏宁易购

台山冲蒌镇的前锋村是一条贫困村,村民基本以农耕为主。村民耕种出来的稻谷如何卖得好,一直是一个"老大难"问题。由于受海水倒灌、盐碱地较多的影响,村集体收入一直没有起色。三年前,江门市扶贫开发"双到"工作组驻村扶贫后,想方设法为村民解决农产品销路问题。

台山冲蒌镇前锋村扶贫工作组组长谭俊彦发现,不少村民并没有发挥主观能动性。为此扶贫工作组请来了一位"80后"村长廖杰良。"80后"村长廖杰良早年外出打工,一直想用在外打工的经验把家乡建设好。他发现,前锋村1800人一共有1700亩水稻,人均水稻不足1亩,除此之外,村里还有1300亩香蕉林,280亩森林。而村子里除了老人和小孩外,60%的年轻人都出门务工。廖杰良说,"农产品是贫困户主要的收入来源,解决到它的销路的话,基本上就可以解决(贫困户)的大部分收入了。"

通过政府牵线搭桥,苏宁易购中华特色馆台山馆的运营团队来到了前锋村,将该村的1700白亩水稻全部打包收购,解决了村民们卖粮难的后顾之忧。苏宁易购中华特色馆台山馆运营负责人何恒庆说："江门2015年也发生过这个马铃薯滞销的问题，启发了我们启动中华特色馆台山馆农产品的销售的初衷，加上台山扶贫的宗旨和目的，希望苏宁易购台山馆能解决台山贫困村农产品滞销的问题。"

除了线上苏宁台山馆，台山市还在线上推出了"扶贫APP"。"扶贫APP"最大限度集纳了贫困村、贫困户的信息以及针对他们开展精准扶贫的多种活动和形式，突破了传统帮扶模式，今后一系列线上线下的低成本帮扶活动均可通过此渠道渐次展开。

该款APP软件近期首个帮扶活动是"爱心菜篮"，置于"公益众筹"模块中。其形式是以当前台山市920户贫困户所种植的优质农产品为扶贫产品，推出"爱心99幸福菜篮"（取"爱心久久"之义）1000份，每份99元，所得收益全部给贫困户，以解决他们的销售困境。

网上求职"通道"
铺到家门口

"动动笔，填张报名表，在家里就能等到就业的机会，省去了很多麻烦。"近日，河头镇湾中村贫困户练成健家里收到了这样的"工作报名表"。新兴县推进精准扶贫精准脱贫、引入人力资源实时招聘平台——淘力网络科技有限公司（以下简称"淘力"），并根据贫困户实际情况，"量身定制"了"网上求职申请表格"。

根据驻村扶贫干部的指引，练成健完善了个人信息、工作经验及就业意向等简历情况。练成健说，驻村扶贫干部会帮助他把简历上传至淘力平台进行职位匹配，平台也将通过手机客户端把工作信息推送到他手中，"一旦匹配成功，就能参加应聘了"。

练成健22岁，刚刚大专毕业，"求职难"是他毕业以来最大的感受。相比之下，由驻村干部协助录入个人信息，通过淘力平台实时求职，等待匹配职位和应聘，比起在各招聘网站盲目地投简历，要省去各种不必要的麻烦，也更容易获得就业机会。

对此，练成健举了一个例子：毕业之后，他为了找工作，曾通过各种招聘网站、手机软件投递简历达100多份，但由于学历不高，缺乏相应的工作经验，求职之路屡屡碰壁。如今，他在广州某公司工作，实习期工资2300元，扣除日常生活所需的花销，所剩无几。

练成健说，他希望能通过淘力平台获得一份更好的工作，对于工资福利薪酬，期望能达到3000元或以上。"如果月薪能达到3000元或以上，我就能节省更多的钱寄回家里，让家里尽快摆脱贫困状态。"

经过全面核查，截至6月底，新兴县共核准相对贫困户7054户16681人，而要实现全面脱贫，首要解决的就是2446户9569人有劳动能力的贫困户的就业问题，帮助贫困户通过就业实现脱贫。

然而，受制于地理位置、交通不便、信息滞后等因素，贫困户找工作，大都只能依靠亲戚朋友介绍，到城市找工作往往费时费力不讨好。帮助贫困户就业，成为三年精准扶贫的重点和难点。新兴县引入的淘力平台采取"互联网+劳动力就业"的模式，面向全部建档立卡贫困户劳动力，以淘力平台互联网O2O模式运作，通过手机客户端将工作岗位信息推送到贫困户手中。同时，贫困户还可通过淘力职业技术培训提高技能，找到更好的工作，获得更高的收入。

新兴县扶贫办工作人员张志军介绍，为了创造更多的就业机会，新兴县与淘力就业平台签订了合作协议，淘力也为此专门成立新兴县精准扶贫项目组，双方就如何为贫困户提供就业岗位的推介和职业培训的项目进行了多次研究。

考虑到个别贫困户没有智能手机，淘力专门为其设置和印制纸质工作报名表，这样，贫困户通过报名表，由驻村干部协助贫困户通过手机客户端"淘力实时招聘平台"实时求职，也可以由贫困户自行通过手机客户端录入个人信息资料即时求职。

日前，新兴县扶贫办组织15个重点村的驻村干部、第一书记等召开新兴县精准脱贫"劳动力就业扶贫工程"培训暨工作推进会。年内，淘力公司将为贫困户提供多个工作岗位，如面向18~50岁女性提供家政服务岗位，面向18~50岁贫困户提供技工、普工、仓库管理、品质检验、焊接工、电工等工作岗位。

高铁改变了
的大山生活

高铁带来人气、财气

初夏的贵州，清风和煦，阳光灿烂，一片片翠绿的茶园里，茶农像往年一样在茶园里忙碌着。而在贵广高铁另一头的广东，一台台电脑正在飞速上网，联系着茶叶的销路。这样的改变与往年不同，科技信息与交通设施越发发达，贵州的茶农茶商和广东的茶叶批发商们，正乘着互联网大数据这朵"云"，不断提升贵州茶叶质量安全公信度，用互联网做大茶产业；同时，借着贵广高铁开通、融入珠三角3小时经济圈的"东风"，茶山扶贫经济正在崛起。

铁路作为国民经济大动脉、国家重要基础设施和大众化交通工具，多年来，铁路部门在确保人们安全便捷出行的同时，也在沿途的贫困地区扶贫开发和区域经济协调发展上发挥了重要作用。"铁路一通，黄金万两"，中国的这一说法就是表明铁路作为打通各地经济命脉的连接线的重要性。

1998年，广梅汕铁路（连接广州、梅州和汕头）开通初期，沿线龙川、五华、兴宁、丰顺等县均是"国家级贫困县"，到2016年，这几县全部走出了"国家级贫困县"序列。随着广州至梅州至汕头铁路提速扩能、惠梅汕高铁建设逐步铺开，沿线地区将再次迎来发展良机。

　　与此同时，2009年开通的武广高铁（武汉至广州）途经区域已经"隆起"了一条"大产业带"。武广高铁2009年开通迄今6年，沿途的韶关、清远以及湘鄂高铁沿线城市共承接珠三角产业转移项目10000多个，总投资突破5000亿元。2015年，清远、韶关等高铁沿线城市的GDP增长率均在8%以上，增幅高出全省其他各市，均较无高铁前的2008年高了5个百分点。

列车上曾经的"动物园"

历时18个多小时，经过857千米，这是以往从贵州开往广东的列车专线的时间和距离。从上个世纪开始，贵州和广东的"慢列车"已经运行了近半个世纪。常年穿梭于这个列车上的刘文成回忆道，通常在火车的最后一节车厢——行李车厢，许多乘客会围在一起。旁边堆放着几个装满活鸡的大背篓。对于61岁的刘文成来说，这条线他再熟悉不过了。

20年前，他就是坐这趟车把贵州山上收集的茶叶带到广东售卖。20年后，他依旧在靠着这条铁路增收致富。每隔半个月，这位老人便会和三五伙伴一起，背着收好的茶叶，步行1个多小时，赶在13时01分之前登上驶往广东的火车。每斤20元收，30元卖。除去车费，刘文成一次可以赚上500多元。

每年卖茶叶的几千元收入，已经成为他家庭收入的重要补充。"火车方便、票价低，我们才能赚到钱。"刘文成讲述时，对铁路给他带来的便利心满意足。

在20多年前，除了茶叶，车厢远处，成群的鸭鹅，叫声此起彼伏，几只山羊在车厢里互相争斗，俨然一派"动物园"的场景。说话间，一只鹅下了个蛋，引得满堂哄笑。

早在20多年前，为了方便沿线贵州少数民族村民携带牲口赶集贸易，贵州部分列车专门打造了"行李车厢"安置牲口和大件行李，沿途车站还配备了专供牲口上下车使用的梯子。穿行在这儿的扶贫"慢列车"，已经成为拉动沿线经济发展和百姓生活的重要"引擎"。

如今，"慢列车"消失了，"行李车厢"的使命也早已告一段落，现在连接贵州和广东的是一条时速高达350公里的高速铁路，贵州和广州的两省生活从21个小时变成了5个半小时。

从"顿顿红苕包谷饭，吃水要翻几匹山"到"吃水不用抬，做饭不烧柴"，40多年"低头种茶"让贵州省湄潭县核桃坝村逐渐脱离了贫困。随着贵广高铁的开通，从"修大坝、种茶园、户户通马路"到"创品牌、搞联合、互联网营销"，短短数年间，原本只会"抬头看天"的茶农，现在已经把眼光瞄向更广的市场。

从种茶到收购茶青、加工制茶，从事茶产业10多年的湄潭县湄江镇核桃坝村茶农景林波除了拥有自己的茶叶公司外，还建起了占地近6亩的制茶作坊。

但靠零售和批发为主的茶生意并不能让这位30来岁的年轻人满意。每斤茶叶去掉成本，也就赚十几、二十元钱加工费，还经常被压价，没啥利润空间，景林波认为，需要从低端往上走，景林波将目光放在了塑造品牌上。景林波决心打造自己的品牌。随着贵广高铁的开通，交通运输成本大大降低，随着人流、物流的你来我往，茶农们终于挣脱了交通不便带来的困境，核桃坝村也开始走出贫困。

湄潭县是贵州主要茶产区，种植面积50多万亩，2014年茶叶综合收入超过30亿元。作为湄潭县茶产业、茶文化的源头，核桃坝村更是"因茶而兴"。全村1万多亩茶园，868户村民家家户户种茶或加工茶，早就名扬茶界的核桃坝茶叶更是被广东的茶商大量收购。

2014年，当地农民人均纯收入达到了1.42万元，但越来越多的茶农不再满足于做产业链条中利润最少的一环，互联网成了茶农开拓市场的"利器"。从2014年年底开始，茶农刘声彦就一直忙着开发微信订阅号、服务号，传送"芸香茶叶"相关资讯，通过美文美图传播，让更多的人知晓湄潭绿茶。目前，核桃坝村已有几十家企业在天猫、京东等大型电商网站上建立了自己的网络销售渠道，销售额逐年提高。

如何把种茶变成产业，让自己从茶农蜕变为茶商？茶农刘泽远打算联合村里的茶叶加工大户，成立一家茶叶"聚集公司"，联手实现不压价、不赊账，以解决投资成本少、资金回笼慢等经营难题。如今，县里每年都会带领大批茶农、生产企业参加国内的各类农产品交易会、茶叶博览会等以便寻找商机。

高铁精准扶贫为
特殊旅客免费

　　2017年1月18日，广州南至百色D3782、广州南至贵阳北D2812、深圳北至武汉G1010、深圳西至吉首K9064等4趟"幸福列车"满载着3000多名旅客，先后从广州和深圳发出，奔赴桂黔鄂湘4省份。这些旅客身份有些特殊，他们分别是创客一族、往年的"摩托大军"以及精准扶贫对象。

　　周刚毅是"指舞互动"VR游戏开发团队合伙人之一。他们共同开发了炫酷的VR产品，如"神游敦煌莫高窟"等。在高铁上，周刚毅的演示引起了很多人的关注。他说："每个年轻人都有创业的梦想，现在国家政策这么好，只要踏实去做，就一定有成功的可能。"

　　湖南省吉首市、广西壮族自治区百色市、贵州省贵阳市均为广东省的对口扶贫地区。从深圳到吉首的K9064次普铁也是参与扶贫的专列。春运前夕，广铁集团联合媒体发布招募信息，重点招募湖南吉首、花垣县十八洞村及其周边在广东务工的建档立卡扶贫对象、技工院校贫困学生、在粤贫困务工青年，由广东省人社厅和爱心企业赠送返乡专列火车票。广铁安排吉首籍铁路列车员担当值乘服务任务，并在列车上举行爱心活动。

　　担当列车服务工作的铁路职工梁永宁是残障人士，也是"宝贝回家"公益组织发起人之一，曾获评"微博2016十大影响力公益大V"。他以个人名义捐助10张火车票帮助十八洞村建档立卡扶贫对象回家过年。获得免费车票之一的段光明是一名退伍军人，经对口帮扶在深圳一家电子厂上班，一个月收入能有5000元左右，家里情况逐步改善。

　　广州南至贵州、百色的2趟高铁扶贫专列上，服务群体不仅有在广东务工的建档立卡扶贫对象，还有每年需要扶助关爱的"摩托大军"。由于广东和广西、贵州各地摩托车限行越来越普遍，贵广南广高铁运力2016年春运提升了20%，每天可以运输7万名旅客，因此在延续2015年春运开行摩托大军返乡专列的基础上，2016年继续开行爱心高铁专列，让更多"摩托大军"回家之路更为安全、舒适。

特色小镇：
其实大山里
也很好

广州"北大荒"变身

吕田镇莲麻村位于广州市最北部,这里北邻韶关市新丰县,东临惠州市龙门县,被誉为广州的"北大门"。近年来,空气清新、宁静优美的自然环境让莲麻村的旅游资源被"盯"上,大力发展莲麻村被纳入从化区"美丽小镇"建设项目之一,莲麻村已经摇身一变,让许多人不再认识当年的贫困村。随着"美丽小镇"的变化,大山里的日子越来越好,在不久的将来,大山的日子反而成为城市人们向往的生活。

莲麻村共有11个经济社,人口1406人,是广州市面积最大的一条行政村。莲麻村以山地为主,由于受到地形因素限制,这里不适宜种植一般的蔬菜,农作物以三华李、沙糖桔为主。"过去,村民收入主要来源于经济林,后来由于国家出台大力保护森林资源的政策,村经济收入以林业为主的传统模式被打破。村民只能靠水源保护林的保护经费作为收入,并且很多有劳动能力的村民都选择外出务工。"莲麻村党支部书记潘光灶说。由于该村地处偏远,农民经济来源少,过去曾经被从化当地人称为嫁女都嫌弃的"北大荒"。

吕田镇最北部的莲麻村的贫困状况萦绕在镇、村干部心头，如何有效整合利用现有资源，走出一条属于自己村的发展之路，在他们的心中打上了问号。2014年底，广州市领导到莲麻村调研，给莲麻村指出发展生态旅游的方向，带来了新的机遇。2015年，从化区决定把莲麻村打造成"美丽小镇"，这个契机如同春风一般给莲麻村带来了改革的温度，使之在一年多的时间里遍地开满了改革之花。从2013年7月开始，广州开展了对莲麻村进行了三年多的帮扶，使该村面貌焕然一新。2016年，经过精准帮扶后的莲麻村集体收入达到56.53万元，村中20户贫困户家庭人均年收入达到1.5万元以上，摇身一变成为被周围村镇羡慕的"北大仓"。

"美丽小镇"的建设给莲麻村带来了翻天覆地的改变，村民纷纷表示，他们能感受到最直观的变化是村容村貌改善了，村民收入增加了。

基础设施建设乃是最大的民生工程，莲麻村的改造提升亦是从最基本的惠民设施建设开始。潘光灿介绍，近一年来，莲麻村逐渐形成了美丽乡村建设规模，基础设施建设发生了很大变化，包括道路、河堤、绿道、停车场、污水设施等都在如火如荼建设当中，目前已完成了4公里的河堤建设和12公里的绿道建设，而从G105线到莲麻村黄沙坑经济社共3.1公里长的社道已改造成沥青路。在环境方面，村委附近一带增加了不少园林绿化景观，带来了耳目一新的景象。

农民变身民宿"掌柜"

现在，从广州经高速可直达莲麻村附近，高速公路的陆续贯通为这座北部山区农村带来人气及商业机会。2016年9月，广州华夏职业学院投资建设的大学生艺术旅馆在莲麻村正式动工。该项目计划历时3个月，总投资600万元，通过盘活闲置农舍打造现代和生态特色合一的艺术基地，促进当地农村经济发展。

艺术旅馆工地不远处，民宿建设正火热进行。在村委旁边，一家名叫"岚坞"的民宿尤其显眼。走进这家民宿，处处充满农家的自然气息，漂亮而又不失乡间乐趣。这是村民陈惠春的家改造而成的莲麻村首家民宿。

自2015年底试业以来，陈惠春家的民宿受到游客欢迎。过往，陈惠春只是一名普通的农家主妇，日常在家种菜打理家务。而今，因应"莲麻小镇"的快速发展，她当起了"掌柜"，获得一份固定收入。

吕田镇相关负责人表示，政府支持农户建设民宿农家乐，首期将选择10家作为试点，财政资金适度支持，采取"政府+村集体+农户"的合作模式来打造。这些村民民宿农家乐都将由村集体筹建的广州北景源旅游开发有限公司统一规划管理，这样可以避免莲麻民宿农家乐陷于无序发展和恶性竞争。

除了民宿，以都市农业、文化旅游为特色的花生油土作坊、广州美院画家创作旅馆等都在火热建设中。其中，能接待300名游客的莲麻会务中心及青年旅社将在2017年完工启用。眼下，陈惠春正和村民商议，扩大民宿的经营范围，抢占国庆商机。"未来，将会有更多的特色文旅设施在莲麻涌现。"她憧憬道。

与莲麻河并行向北的古驿道留存至今只剩下300米，村委会翻查过明清资料，按照历史书卷只言片语的描绘加以修缮。村支书潘光灶期望，翻新的古驿道能够"说出"旧时的莲麻故事。"引进项目并不意味着大拆大建，立足莲麻传统，原汁原味保留乡村生态特色是'莲麻小镇'的建设理念。"吕田镇相关负责人表示，早在建设之初，就专门邀请中国乡村建设院团队到访，并一同打磨"莲麻小镇"规划建设方案，呈现乡村特色成为主要焦点。

"莲麻土法豆腐和土榨花生油远近驰名，是当地的特色农产品，引进企业以工业化的手段帮助农民升级生产力，不仅是扩大生产，更重要的是展现农村的传统工艺。"他透露，目前，白酒作坊已邀请五粮液大师前来教学，提炼酿酒的文化价值。

从化商人罗霆近年寻求新产业的投资机遇，十多年没有回家乡的他在今年春节来到了莲麻，"小镇建设如火如荼，满地都是机遇"。商业嗅觉灵敏的罗霆在春节决心回到家乡，投资都市农业。

第一步是翻新农舍，邀请设计师规划建设农家乐；第二步是发展绿色庄园，与村民合作"试水"规模种植、养殖，发展当地特色的都市农业。从传统钢铁贸易转身"掘金"现代农业的罗霆在莲麻找到了传统资本向新业态转型的附着点，而借助广州最北得天独厚的生态环境，越来越多像罗霆这样的投资者把资本向莲麻的优质生态资源靠拢。目前，莲麻村引进了多家企业，来自流溪河源头的绿色农产品和农家文化产品将走向珠三角。

创客进村加速"小镇"建设

　　国庆假期临近，80后女青年潘安娜需要在莲麻周边走访，加紧准备物料，以应对国庆的人流高峰。2006年大学毕业后，潘安娜先后在镇政府等单位就职。2015年底，她选择扎根莲麻村，筹建她人生的第一个创业项目——"北源之家"。

　　"北是指广州最北，源是流溪河源头的意思，我们希望能给顾客家一般的温暖。"潘安娜投资不多，她先从盘活泥砖屋起步，通过装修和修缮，把农舍装扮一新。

　　2015年底经营至今，"北源之家"在互联网上小有名气，而通过"北源之家"的住宿和服务，游人们对莲麻有了更深刻的认识。潘安娜说，作为小本经营的创客，她把每月的盈利都滚动投到旅馆和周边建设，比如为小溪增加护栏，铺设青砖，一点一点完善周边的设施。

　　生态旅游、现代农业"搅动"农村产业新脉动，绿色经济带来的发展机遇让年轻人重新回流莲麻村。"现在得知特色小镇发展火热，越来越多年轻人进村寻求机遇，里面既有年轻村民，也有学生，还有一些创业人士。"潘光灶说，光是出外打工回流的本村青年就有十几户，人口结构的变化为这座山区农村注入新活力，小镇建设正在提速。

任何的改革都并非一帆风顺，对于莲麻村发生的改变，村民的不理解源于不了解，村民的支持则源于切身感受到改变带来的实惠。潘光灶说，莲麻村的发展定位是打造生态旅游景区，因此，配套建设民宿、农家乐和乡村酒店是莲麻村今后一个时期的重要项目之一。随着宣传效应带来的影响力，莲麻村宁静清新的自然环境吸引了很多游客前来一探究竟。潘光灶介绍："目前，我村已开业的农家乐共有三家，每逢周六日或者公众假期，到这里来吃农家菜和住宿的游客特别多，其中一家从春节到现在，已经获得10万元的收入。"2016年一月份，大广高速的开通给莲麻村带来了很大的影响，在村委干部的争取下，大广高速地派出口增加了"莲麻村"的字眼，这大大增加了莲麻村的知名度。从地派出口下高速，只需要经过5公里的国道就可以抵达莲麻村，如今，从广州城区到莲麻村只需要80分钟的车程，十分方便快捷。在2016年"五一"假期，莲麻村的农家乐入住率爆满，供不应求。

为鼓励村民大力支持家乡的建设发展，提高村民的创业积极性，村委还制定了优惠政策，率先投入建设民宿、农家乐的前十户将获得5万元的赞助款。目前莲麻村正在开展的大大小小项目中，涉及人力、机械设备等资源的，在同等条件下，将会优先考虑该村村民，为他们带来就业机会，增加村民收入。

从化特色小镇成
区域创新"新引擎"

　　2016年11月最后一个周末，广州首届稻草节在从化西塘村拉开帷幕。本届稻草节主题不仅是生态旅游和休闲观光，更是动漫协会和西塘童话小镇的首度"牵手"——动漫元素走进童话小镇核心区的开始。早前，国家体育总局有关部门与从化区正式签订"全国户外产业示范区"合作协议，未来五年，包括广州露营大会、户外运动节、全国登山健身大会等大型赛事及活动陆续落地特色小镇。在品牌活动引领下，来自全国的人流、信息流、资金流等要素将与从化产生连接。

　　秋收后，从化鳌头镇西塘村遍地是金色的稻田。每年11月底，当地人就把稻草做成简单的稻草人供村民娱乐。2016年稻草节升级成为全市规模的大型活动，为西塘村带来庞大的人流和商机。

　　西塘村位于鳌头镇东北部，S355线道旁，面积约4.2平方公里，东距从化城区11公里，南距广州市区60公里，全村耕地有1998亩。旧时的西塘村发展滞后，村里大部分青壮年都外出务工。

　　2015年底，西塘村纳入从化特色小镇建设中，并定义为"童话小镇"。如何把童话变为现实？"首先是基础设施建设、村容环境整治，其次是引进企业注入发展的内生动力，最后是动漫元素和资源的进驻。"鳌头镇有关负责人表示。

"西塘生态资源丰富，打通生态到产业的通道，为农村注入发展活力，是当地人最殷切的期望。"西塘村支书陈海涛说，2016年初，西塘村先后引进3家都市型农业企业，几个月前，陆续有村民回流寻找就业机遇，昔日冷清的农村顿时热闹起来。30名本地村民变身为大棚工人，他们每天需要管理好蔬菜，并按照需求匹配蔬菜到不同的家庭包裹里，最后通过冷链配送到广州200个家庭。

"西塘稻草节背后实际上是搭建平台打出小镇知名度，引进更多企业，融合动漫文化发展以'三农'为核心内容的童话旅游小镇。"从化区有关负责人透露策划稻草节幕后的"野心"。

西塘村2016年19个特色小镇建设项目已全部进入实施阶段。稻草节后，西塘将迎来新一轮的改造，未来还将整合资源建设"种子王国""昆虫王国"，为前来发展的动漫企业提供写生及触发灵感的生态科普地。

宝趣玫瑰世界、樱花园、万花园，多个生态旅游景区，数片灿烂花海，将西和村勾勒成一幅极具风情的画作。在特色小镇建设项目的带动下，政府推动退果还田和土地流转，吸引企业落户。西和村负责人说，当地大棚生产的高产值、高附加值的农业生产结构模式，实现了花卉生产产业化，提高了土地的种植效益。目前，西和美丽小镇已进驻35家企业，已投入生产面积1万多亩，初步形成以生产鲜切花、兰花、盆花、樱花、特色苗木为主体的花卉生产及观光产业。

"西和村要打造成广州最具风情的小镇，建设广东唯一的特色农业公园。"从化城郊街道相关负责人介绍。从北部吕田到温泉再到南部城郊，几个特色小镇初步成型，串珠成链展现出不同以往的面貌。

目前，从化通过论证调研，已形成以露营和徒步为特色的广州最北的莲麻小镇；依托花卉特色资源打造成岭南花海于一体的西和风情小镇；以特色金融、创业创新、婚庆浪漫为产业的温泉财富小镇；以童话为主题针对儿童及亲子市场打造西塘童话小镇。

到2020年广东拟建成
百个省级特色小镇

特色小镇是指在城镇（城市）的特定区域，以特色产业集聚发展为特征，融合产业、文化、旅游、生活等功能的新型发展空间。

广东将以特色主导产业和经典产业为重点，打造九大特色小镇。特色小镇要突出一个"特"字，产业有特色，特色小镇的形态也要"特"。

同时，特色小镇还是促进创新创业，在国内同样推广建设特色小镇的浙江，特色小镇促进有效投资、激活消费热情的效果已然显现。以东莞市松山湖为例，据介绍，当地正努力建设"互联网+"小镇，结合自身产业特点，积极完善小镇创新创业生态，互联网特色产业集群初具规模。到2018年，小镇将建成220万平方米的创业基地，力争培育3~5家互联网产业龙头企业、500家互联网创新型中小企业。

图书在版编目（CIP）数据

共享的广东 / 王鹤著. —广州：广东人民出版社，2017.6
（中国梦·广东故事）
ISBN 978-7-218-11892-5

Ⅰ. ①共… Ⅱ. ①王… Ⅲ. ①农村—社会主义建设—研究 Ⅳ. ①F327.65

中国版本图书馆CIP数据核字（2017）第129134号

GONGXIANG DE GUANGDONG

共享的广东　　王　鹤　著

出　版　人：肖风华

总　撰　稿：刘　旦
责任编辑：王　宁　施　勇
封面设计：李桢涛
责任技编：周　杰　吴彦斌

出版发行：广东人民出版社
地　　址：广州市大沙头四马路10号（邮政编码：510102）
电　　话：（020）83798714（总编室）
传　　真：（020）83780199
网　　址：http://www.gdpph.com
印　　刷：广东信源彩色印务有限公司
开　　本：787mm×1092mm　1/32
印　　张：6.5　字　数：200千
版　　次：2017年6月第1版　2017年6月第1次印刷
定　　价：60.00元

如发现印装质量问题，影响阅读，请与出版社（020-83795749）联系调换。
售书热线：（020）83795240